DEDICATION

FOR MY BELOVED FRIENDS, MICHAEL AND STEVEN RUSSELL.

MAY THE GIFT OF OUR MEETING IN THIS LIFETIME BRING THE GIFT OF HEALING TO MANY OTHERS.

WITH ALL MY LOVE —

Caroline

AIDS: PASSAGEWAY TO TRANSFORMATION

C. NORMAN SHEALY, M.D., Ph.D.
CAROLINE M. MYSS, M.A.

FIRST EDITION

This book is manufactured in the United States of
America. Cover design by Diane DePaolis.
Text design by Diane DePaolis and Elizabeth Doherty.
Published by Stillpoint Publishing, a division of
Stillpoint International, Inc.,
Box 640, Meetinghouse Road, Walpole, NH 03608

Published simultaneously in Canada by
Fitzhenry & Whiteside Ltd., Toronto

Library of Congress Card Catalog Number: 87-062669
9 8 7 6 5 4 3 2 1

A Stillpoint CREATION OF HEALTH SERIES © Book

TABLE OF CONTENTS

FOREWORD

As this century winds down, medicine as we know it is being redefined. This may be inapparent to those persons within and without the profession who remain focused on the traditional concepts of disease and therapy. But for those who can catch the main drifts, it is clear that our medical world can never be the same. It is not, and can never be, business as usual.

This work by Shealy and Myss is a part of the emerging model of humans. If there is a single, dominant feature of this new view, it is this: consciousness—whatever we may mean by that term—matters. It matters greatly, not just in trivial, relatively inconsequential ways, as many psychosomatic theorists have maintained. It is no exaggeration to say that one's state of mind not only contributes to health and illness; it can be a matter of life and death.

This fact is most vividly dramatized in the area of cardio-vascular medicine, where life-threatening events can occur within seconds. In other areas the effects of the mind work more slowly—as in the immune system, which is the territory being explored by Shealy and Myss. Because of the larger time scales involved, which may be on the order of months or even years, and because, also, of the astounding number of intermediary variables involved, such as whole families of immune cells, microorganisms, antigens and antibodies, and hormones, the effects of the human mind may seem dwarfed or completely overshadowed. But they are there if we look in astute ways. And in immune-related disorders the effects of mind, too, may be a matter of life or death.

Yes, we have argued for centuries about these issues. What is the mind? Is it really something different from the brain and body? Can the mind really "do" anything? How can something as vaporous and immaterial as "consciousness" affect something concrete, such as the material body? These questions will continue to vex our philosophers, as they ought. But today, for the sake of humanity, we must leapfrog all the philosophical indecision about these matters and proceed on the basis of what we observe in real-life situations. Regardless of what our philosophers wish to say about what the mind is, and what it can and cannot do, the fact remains that particular states of consciousness are correlated decisively with particular states of health and illness. Thus, while our philosophers philosophize and our theorists theorize about the nature of the mind, we are killing ourselves—with our minds.

If the new "mental factor" in medicine sounds new, it is not. Today it is still true that when most people fall ill, they are treated with some form of therapy which relies on the effects of the mind. In most places there are no modern hospitals, and folk healers and shamans still account for most of the medicine practiced on the face of the earth. These techniques, while they employ various esoteric methods, rely heavily on the powers of consciousness of the healer and the healee. The power of the mind has been the veritable backbone of shamanism, whose history extends for 50,000 years. From this perspective we are treading old paths. We are rediscovering ancient truths about ourselves which we have almost forgotten in an age of science.

But our knowledge about the importance of the mind in health and illness is scientific as well. It is important to realize this fact, for many persons believe the conclusions which

Shealy and Myss have reached are simply unsubstantiated musings which have no basis in fact. This is hardly the case. In fact, an entirely new field in medicine has arisen in the past decade, called psychoneuroimmunology—PNI—which asserts that the psyche, the neurological system, and the immune system are intricately connected in our bodies. And not just these systems, but the cardiovascular, gastrointestinal, pulmonary, and probably any other system in the body comes under the influence of human consciousness, at least to some degree. Today the effects of human consciousness are a matter of record. They are hardly a production of the psychic and the seer.

That is not to say that the psychic's insights should be disregarded. Indeed, they must be taken seriously and evaluated via the rigid, unforgiving rules of scientific inquiry. That is what makes Myss's contribution to this book so intriguing. Her insights into the "victimization" concept as a predisposing psychological pattern for the clinical expression of AIDS fit with much of the known data in other disease categories dealing with the relationship of psychological states and specific diseases. There is much information already which shows the devastating effects of social isolation, fear, depression and failure to externalize emotion—which are just those qualities singled out by Shealy and Myss as pathological.

Moreover, Myss's means of gaining information—making "psychic diagnoses" at a distance on persons she has never seen—must also be taken seriously. This, no doubt, will cause an enormous degree of intellectual indigestion in those who are dedicated to certain ideas about how the mind "ought" to behave. Yet the record cannot be doctored, and the facts will not go away: it is possible for the mind to violate the constraints of linear time and spatial separation, and gain information in non-ordinary ways. There is an impressive array of data from the work of physicists Puthoff and Targ at Stanford Research Institute on remote sensing, and by Dean Emeritus of the School of Engineering at Princeton University, Robert Jahn, showing that quite ordinary people can gain information when they are widely separated from the source of such information, and—which is most surprising—before such information has even been transmitted. This data, as C.G. Jung once pointed out, is much easier to ignore than to explain. But regardless of the conceptual problems it may cause, it is there; it must be dealt with, even if it forces us to acknowledge that persons may be able to make "psychic diagnoses" at a distance.

Many people in science already know this. There are emerging models of reality afoot which take these properties of the mind into consideration. As a single example, Professor Emeritus of physics at Yale, Henry Margenau, has proposed that the mind is trans-temporal, trans-spatial, and immaterial; that it is not confined to specific individuals and cannot therefore be merely a product of the brain; and that there is a larger, collective mind, of which all individual minds are a part. This soaring view of human consciousness is set forth in his book *The Miracle of Existence* (Boston: New Science Library, 1987), and should be required reading for any serious student of the human mind. The model Professor Margenau sets forth is not the product of random thoughts, but is consistent with considerations flowing from modern physics, to which he has made fundamental contributions.

The work of Shealy and Myss is consistent with an emerging view of interconnectedness between all things on our planet. There should not be any doubt of this fact, for it is transparently clear that we are united, if only through the rather macabre facts of nuclear threat and environmental destruction. Here the mind clearly connects us all: certain decisions can carry everything, including the planet, over the brink in a matter of minutes. Consistent with this idea, Myss suggests that the earth is in fact a living, feeling organism much like ourselves; that it has needs; and that it may not tolerate our foolishness much longer. Is AIDS a process of self-cleansing set in motion by planet Earth, as Myss suggests? This possibility should not be dismissed out of hand, for we know that homeostatic, self-righting, purging processes are the way of nature, and that we have offended the natural order in many regrettable ways.

The overriding suggestion confronting the reader in this book, then, is that there is a decided mental quality working behind the scenes in AIDS and, indeed, in all phenomena; and that we will never come to a full understanding of the origin of the disease AIDS, nor to a fully adequate form of treatment, without taking into account this mental quality which seems so pervasive, not only in our own bodies, but in nature in general.

There is only one point in the book on which I would demur, and it has to do with the recommended treatments. I cannot endorse them officially—not because I know them to be wrong, but because, so far as I know, they have not been subjected to the exacting, rigid rules of science in the form of controlled studies. These rules are rather unforgiving. And while they are sometimes inexact, and may be too harsh on occasion, they still offer us valuable ways of testing our therapies. It may well be that the recommended therapies are extremely effective; if so, that is what we shall find when we scrutinize them scientifically. The point, however, is to test them.

The faith in our century has been that eventually we could design a form of medicine that is totally objective. This medicine would be based solely on pure reason and empirical analysis. That mission has failed. The goal was wrong in principle. We know today beyond a shadow of a doubt that medicine can never be totally objective, for objectivity is not the full measure of humans. When it comes to human illness, the situation is much more complex. Here the impact of perceived meanings enters, and we cannot get rid of them. They affect what the body does, what the immune system does, from the perspective of Shealy and Myss. Meanings cannot be given objective status. By definition, they are subjective, and they are tied to the existence of mind and consciousness.

So the question becomes: which meanings make us healthy, and which make us sick? The answers are contained in this book.

LARRY DOSSEY, M.D.

 Dallas, Texas
Author, *SPACE, TIME AND MEDICINE: BEYOND ILLNESS
         and MIND BEYOND BODY* (forthcoming)
August 1987

PREFACE

We are only now beginning to investigate seriously the connection which exists between our emotional, psychological and spiritual selves and the health of our physical bodies. All of us working in this field are, at best, pioneers, studying and wondering about the invisible power of human emotions and the effect this invisible power has upon the visible world of matter—both the "matter" that is our bodies and the "matter" that forms our planet.

It is easy to accept the connection, for instance, between depression and the common cold or between stress and the formation of an ulcer. Yet, when the disease we are looking at is a more complex one, such as cancer, neurological disorders or chronic pain, tracing the emotional threads becomes a higher risk procedure and thus, physical causes are sought as the root of the dysfunction because they are more immediate and more obvious.

Since 1985, I have worked with Norm Shealy, M.D., using clairvoyant abilities to assist Norm in identifying the emotional, psychological and spiritual stress factors within a person's inner world that have contributed to the creation of a physical disease. The data I provide Norm is that which cannot be measured clinically nor determined through blood samples. The process through which we work is simple: Norm calls me at my home in New Hampshire while his patient is in his Springfield, Missouri office. I require only the name and age of a patient and the patient's permission to do the reading. I then share with Norm the information that I intuitively perceive about that patient's life: the emotional stresses around childhood, or relationships, or traumas a person may have endured, such as rape or abandonment. In almost all cases, people's energy fields reveal how they feel about themselves, if they feel powerless in this world, if they are filled with resentments or grief, fears or guilt feelings. The combination of these emotional stresses combined with the INTENSITY of these stresses indicates to me what specific physical dysfunction exists.

We have done hundreds of patient readings and as yet have not found an exception to the pattern that before physical disease is manifested, an individual is existing in an internal climate of tremendous stress. Further, our research indicates that specific patterns of stress create specific diseases. Just as a physician can recognize certain symptoms as indicators of the presence of a specific disease, so, also, do specific emotional, psychological and spiritual stresses indicate the probability of a specific disease.

How does this information contribute to the healing process?

There is a difference between treating an illness and the complete healing of a disease. Drugs and surgery "treat" a disease, but are they capable of healing grief or memories that plague a person's mind? Are drugs able to heal the heart-break of the death of a spouse or a child? In addition to the physical treatments which are provided by the medical world, people need to heal the parts of their lives that are pain-filled. This is the dimension of healing that requires a great amount of courage on the part of the patient because it is not easy to confront that which is not working in our lives. When the pain is intense enough, this process of confrontation with the self is more appropriately recognized as the journey of complete transformation.

Healing AIDS requires a complete transformation of one's life. The emotional, psychological and spiritual stresses that exist within the experience of this disease penetrate the whole of one's life.

AIDS: Passageway to Transformation examines the human factors that, according to our research, seem to be characteristic of those people who are, and have been, most susceptible to the HTLV-III/IV virus. Norm and I believe our work adds a substantial contribution toward understanding the human elements—as well as the physical factors—that make a physical body a receptor for a particular virus. We do not claim to have penetrated completely the mystery of AIDS. We share in this book what has been our personal experience in working with people who have AIDS in the hope that this becomes one more valuable piece of information that can be contributed to the body of material now being gathered around the world. We do believe that our contribution provides a serious step forward in understanding the intimate connection that exists between the experience of AIDS and the state of health of our minds, our bodies and our spirits.

Perhaps the boldest information contained in this material is the thesis that the planet itself has AIDS, and that epidemics of any kind have a direct connection to the emotional, psychological and spiritual health of groups of people, even if the "group" identified is an entire nation. This level of perception—connecting the experiences of individuals to the experience of the larger life-body of the planet—represents a perceptual range of thinking we are only now, as a species, able to grapple with intelligently. The idea that "what is in one is in the whole" may well be emerging as a fundamental principle of life.

In our next book, *The Creation of Health*, Norm and I will examine the link of other major illnesses, such as cancer and chronic pain, to the greater planetary body. This is mentioned here as a point of clarity, because AIDS is not unique in its relationship to the greater whole of the planet. We have, however, limited our material in this book solely to examining the factors which embody the AIDS epidemic.

May this book become a tool of hope for all of us seeking a higher order of reasoning for the difficulties we are all facing as members of the same planetary family.

Caroline M. Myss
Walpole, NH 1987

Caroline has said it so well that I have little to add. I am drawn to work on the AIDS problem because it is probable that our world will face panic as the epidemic spreads. In encountering AIDS patients, physicians and health professionals must face their own fears and prejudices. Homophobia and fear of death are the most important considerations.

In recommending a treatment plan, I have relied upon intuition as well as therapeutic approaches which have at least some evidence that they enhance immune function. And they fulfill my most crucial requirement of safety. For a disease where there is no known scientific "cure," it seems reasonable to use techniques which have been demonstrated effective in enhancing immune health or immune strength, especially when they are safe. We are eager to find more "white crows" (the name we're giving to people who follow a success-oriented healing program for AIDS; note section entitled *White Crows*) and hope that our thoughts will assist that transformation process for other AIDS patients.

C. Norman Shealy, M.D., Ph.D.
Springfield, Missouri, 1987

INTRODUCTION (Myss)

In 1985, Norm Shealy and I began to work together, combining our skills in order to understand further the nature of health and of disease. Norm is a well-known physician and neurosurgeon and the author of several books on health. I am a medical clairvoyant. The abilities that I have permit me to perceive the active emotional, psychological and spiritual stresses within a human being that lead to the development of a physical disease.

During the time that Norm and I have worked together, we have amassed a critical measure of research which provides strong evidence supporting the intimate connection that exists between the activity of the mind and emotions and the health of the physical body. Our method of working together is this: Norm telephones me for a consultation while the patient is in Norm's office. Although I do not physically see the patient, this does not interfere with my ability to perceive his or her physical body. My contribution to Norm's physical diagnosis is to provide information which is specific to the emotional or psychological traumas that have been experienced by the patient, and that exist as the underlying reasons for the development of a physical disease.

These emotional and psychological factors are often overlooked by both patient and physician because, like so many of us, patients and physicians are accustomed to believing that physical illness develops as a result of external causes. Repeatedly, factors of human stress have been found to play a major part in the creation of every disease, whether that be cancer, chronic pain or AIDS. The well-known work of Carl and Stephanie Simonton in cancer, for example, indicates that many people are prone to develop cancer within 18 months of suffering an extreme trauma, such as the loss of a loved one or the loss of a job.

Whereas cancer has been the leading "incurable" threat to human life in this century, that threat has now been replaced by the even more devastating disease called AIDS. Many cancers are cured or put into remission through traditional medical treatment. So far, no form of medical treatment has been found to cure AIDS, or even to come close to arresting the spread of this virus which has the potential of infecting and killing millions of people worldwide within the next several years.

I began working in 1985 with numerous individuals who were, and are, suffering from AIDS. In each of these cases, the emotional and psychological stresses that I observed within each individual were similar, if not identical. Norm and I believe that these findings provide a significant degree of insight into identifying: 1) the type of personality that is most likely to attract AIDS, 2) the reason that AIDS has become a planetary epidemic, and 3) the most appropriate form of protection from and prevention of AIDS.

The fundamental principle that underlies the holistic approach to health, and to life, is that each person's reality is created through the power of his or her own beliefs, attitudes and mental intentions. This perception challenges the assumption that illness or events which occur within our lives happen randomly. Whereas traditional medicine asserts that disease attacks the body like an invasion from an outside source, the holistic approach asserts that illness is created when emotional, psychological and spiritual stresses within a person become overwhelming and that the relationship of specific stresses to specific diseases is intimate and identifiable. Therefore, a knowledge of this relationship is of critical importance to the prevention and healing of diseases and to the maintenance of health.

The dynamics of holism extend beyond the conditions that exist within our personal lives. We also are part of our environment and we exist in an active, continual relationship with our environment. In the same way that we create our individual realities, we participate "collectively" in the creation of events and conditions upon the earth. A collective belief pattern is created when a majority of people recognize the same perception as a "truth."

We can easily recognize humankind's influence, for example, in the "creation" of air and water pollution. Our society shares a "collective" belief that economic concerns are the priority decision-making influence in almost every situation, often-times overshadowing humanitarian and/or ecological interests. Because so many people hold this "collective" belief, it operates as an active current of influence upon political, social and business decision-making policies. As a result, we have "created" a polluted environment because most of us, to some degree, believe that economic gain is more important than the quality of life. Thus, the responsibility for the creation of air and water pollution rests not only with the corporations whose factories release toxins into the air, water and soil, but also with each person whose own life, in whatever way, reflects the same priorities and belief patterns.

 Are epidemics "created" through the same mechanism of collective energy? If emotional, psychological and spiritual stresses break down the individual human body, it follows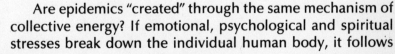

that the same stresses, when endured by a majority of people, create a "collective" illness. The application of holistic thinking would further suggest that the same stresses which influence the quality of human life are simultaneously impacting the quality of all forms of life on this planet, including the planet itself. What is in "one" is indeed in the "whole."

We have applied these principles of holistic thinking to our exploration of AIDS, not only in terms of a recommended approach for healing, but also in investigating the relationship this virus has with our environment and the planet itself. Norm and I believe that AIDS has manifested in our world as a result of specific stress factors shared by a majority of people on this planet, and that the planet itself is experiencing the same stress factors. This material introduces and explores this perception. Because this way of thinking may be unfamiliar to many, we have included background material on previous epidemics to illustrate the points that intense conditions of stress have consistently produced disease, and that the quality of health always has been intimately connected to environmental factors.

PART I:

UNDERSTANDING THE CONSCIOUSNESS OF AIDS

Universality of AIDS

C. Norman Shealy, M.D., Ph.D.

THE SCOPE

AIDS! The simple acronym, which stands for Acquired Immune Deficiency Syndrome, wallops the emotions. We are fearful, repulsed, vexed, confused. The medical profession is confounded. In an age of technical wizardry and remarkable cures, AIDS has the last word: death. The most serious infectious disease known in recorded history, AIDS is an embarrassment to physician and patient alike. Scientific medicine soared in public esteem as it conquered one devastating infectious illness after another: smallpox, measles, diphtheria, whooping cough, poliomyelitis, even some of the elusive influenzas.

According to expert opinion, 92% of medicine's life-saving and life-extending achievements have been focused around infectious diseases. Surprisingly, however, simple measures such as proper handling of sewage, chlorination of water, pasteurization of milk and adequate nutrition have had more of an impact on infectious diseases than the "miracle drugs"—antibiotics. AIDS is not conquered so neatly: the infection disarms the body's immune system, short-circuiting normal protective mechanisms, cursing cell upon cell until its macabre finale.

It is estimated that at least 100 million people will die from AIDS, worldwide, within less than a generation. In the United States, AIDS cases are doubling every 12 months. The National Academy of Science conservatively predicts 270,000 AIDS cases by 1991, with 179,000 deaths and medical costs of 70 billion dollars.

In 1986, 15% of the beds at Saint Vincent's Hospital in New York were occupied by AIDS patients. If the trend continues, the bed occupancy needed for AIDS patients will increase to 30% by the end of 1987; 60% by 1988; over 100% by the end of 1989.

Indeed, nationally, if the present trend continues, the number of AIDS patients would require every available hospital bed in the United States by 1992. There are about 325,000 unoccupied hospital beds now. Some experts expect 10 million AIDS deaths in the United States by the year 2000. AIDS is more than an epidemic; AIDS is a modern plague. In less than 10 years, it has replaced cancer as the most dreaded disease.

Susan Sontag, author of *Illness As Metaphor*, compared the "fantasies inspired by tuberculosis in the last century [with those inspired] by cancer now." She also compared the "responses to a disease thought to be intractable and capricious." She reported further, "Any disease that is treated as a mystery and acutely enough feared will be felt to be morally, if not literally, contagious." The public attitude toward AIDS follows this established pattern. Sontag noted that people would speak of tuberculosis with the same hesitancy in the 1800's as they would speak of cancer in the mid-1900's. With the advent of AIDS, cancer may lose some of its reputation as the "evil, invincible predator."

What causes epidemics? Do stresses occur within a society which create specific environmental conditions that are conducive to the massive spread of a disease? The research of Frederick Cartwright, noted social historian, for example, indicates that a direct connection exists between wars and social stresses on the one hand and the onset of epidemics on the other hand. While Cartwright does not discuss the psychological or emotional stress factors of war, consider the emotional climate of a society during and after its involvement in a war. Figuratively speaking, the air is thick with grief, hostility, sorrow and fear.

Stressful social conditions—the societal traumas that follow massive destruction—have yet to be taken into consideration in determining the origin of epidemics. We are only now learning about the intimate connection which exists between our emotional and psychological health and the health of our physical bodies.

Certainly, epidemics follow wars for reasons of infection, famine and lack of sanitation. If, however, we were to interpret the patterns of history with a holistic understanding that takes into account the emotional and psychological health of societies prior to or accompanying the onset of epidemics, we might discover that epidemics are intimately related to outbreaks of massive social anxiety or depression. Consider that our present society, for example, through which AIDS is spreading rapidly, is very deeply in the midst of a massive emotional/psychological crisis. Symptoms such as the breakdown of family structure, widespread use of drugs and alcohol, increasing rate of suicide amongst teenagers, increasing rate of brutal crimes, increasing rate of emotional breakdowns in people of all ages, all indicate that the emotional/psychological health of our collective consciousness is in jeopardy.

Let us, therefore, examine the occurrence of epidemics in terms of society-wide emotional/psychological stress factors. It may be that epidemics, such as AIDS, are parts of larger patterns through which the collective consciousness of humanity is releasing negativity.

If so, we may be discovering that we participate in a consciousness that is made up of all humanity and that this consciousness of the human species is connected directly to the creation of planetary events—such as wars and epidemics—in the same manner that our individual consciousnesses are connected directly to our physical bodies. AIDS calls us to a new awareness of ourselves, of others and of our responsibilities for each other.

EPIDEMICS: A BRIEF LOOK (Shealy)

According to the book of Exodus, a great plague killed all the unprotected first-born males in Egypt. This is estimated to have occurred about 1500 B.C.E. In Samuel 1, it is reported that a plague struck the Philistines following a war with the Israelites, killing 50,000 people. This is estimated to have happened about 1100 B.C.E.

The "plague" of Athens, 430 B.C.E., followed the Peloponnesian War, killing almost two-thirds of the population, and dooming Athens. It could have been scarlet fever, bubonic plague, typhus, smallpox, measles, or anthrax; but this is not known.

In 79 A.D., Rome suffered its first great epidemic (of unknown cause), which lasted at least 50 years. This epidemic spread through the Mediterranean, killing millions of people. In 161 A.D., Germanic barbarians invaded Rome, spreading a plague which continued intermittently until 1889. In 210 A.D., yet another plague spread throughout Europe and Africa, killing more than 50% of the populations of these continents.

By 590 A.D., the Justinian plague (probably bubonic) killed more people than any other epidemic up to that time. From 1346-1361, Black Death killed approximately 24 million Europeans. Another European pandemic (widespread epidemic) occurred between 1540-1590. The Great Plague of London (bubonic) occurred between 1665-1666, and afterwards, recurrent episodes continued to cause large numbers of deaths.

At the end of the 15th century, syphilis (or its African relative, yaws) invaded Europe, perhaps from the West Indies (which in exchange received measles and tuberculosis). Spreading from Spain throughout Europe and into India on drinking cups as well as through sexual contacts, syphilis killed at least 10 million people.

Typhus is a recurrent disease associated with war, filth and crowding. Typhus ravaged Europe during the Thirty Years War, 1618-1648, and remained endemic into the late 19th century. Typhus also devastated two-thirds of the populations of Russia and France during this time.

Measles first appeared in the 16th century. One-fourth of the native population in Fiji was destroyed by an English-imported outbreak in 1875.

Smallpox created numerous epidemics, particularly destructive to children.

Major 20th century epidemics include influenza (the first influenza epidemic appeared just after World War I) and poliomyelitis. All epidemics can be examined in terms of the society-wide psychological and emotional stresses out of which they spring. Poliomyelitis, however, is an especially graphic example of the relationship between the origin of a disease and society-wide psychological and emotional stresses.

The polio epidemic occurred during and after the Great Depression. The Great Depression economically crippled the United States and most of Europe. Indeed, much of the literature on the Great Depression uses the word "crippled" to describe the economy of the 1930's. Is it a coincidence that a literally "crippling" disease came into being at this time? And note that the first effective polio vaccine was discovered shortly after World War II when the world was economically "recovering."

Considering the now recognized lengthy incubation period of AIDS, and considering also the relentless psychological and emotional stress that the global community has experienced as a result of World War II, the Korean War, the Arab-Israeli War(s), the Iran-Iraq War, the Vietnam War, the Afghan-Russian conflict and the continuous series of revolutions (localized wars) that have filled the gaps between these more major conflicts (such as the Cuban, Nicaraguan and Filipino revolutions, to name a very few), we must now wonder whether this lengthy incubation period of the HTLV-III virus reflects this prolonged period of stress.

Obviously, epidemics do not follow only war. They can occur after natural catastrophes such as droughts, volcanic eruptions, earthquakes and other cataclysmic events. Epidemics can occur anytime there is overcrowding, breakdown in sanitation practices, or a generalized excessive stress. This includes massive (and often-times insidious) chemical, nuclear and radiation pollution; nutritional deprivation—not necessarily starvation, but undernourishment from lack of essential nutrients over a significant period of time; panic, both sudden and chronic, that is triggered by one or a series of events or emotional torments.

The media contributes significantly, and often subliminally, to population-wide stress. People are often unconscious of the pervasive disease that they accumulate as news unfolds day after day in threatening dimensions. A significant percentage of the population, for example, senses that the government is concealing the seriousness of this country's present economic woes. Beyond that, there is a feeling of hopelessness and helplessness to control or correct the problem. The specter of the 1929 economic crash is aroused periodically, fueling public anxiety. Chronic anxiety is a scientifically valid coordinate of organ disease. The opportunistic AIDS virus preys on a vulnerable population. Caroline's concept of emotional distress from a feeling of powerlessness fits harmoniously into this scenario of disease development.

AIDS: THE FIRST EPIDEMIC OF THE NUCLEAR AGE (Myss)

As in the case of previous epidemics, we need to consider that AIDS is manifesting now in response to specific stress factors that are present in our physical and social environment. Unlike the polio epidemic, however, or even the bubonic plague, AIDS is not localized within a nation or a continent. AIDS is an epidemic which is sweeping the globe.

Why? The first cases of AIDS were reported in the 1970's. What are the stress factors related to AIDS which have not been present on our planet prior to the 1970's? First, the threat of nuclear devastation has become a reality – indeed, many say a significantly probable reality. How that continually threatening force factors into our minds and into our lives as we plan for our "futures" is difficult to measure. Nonetheless, the thought that all of our futures are no longer guaranteed has become a very potent fear. We are now all existing within a collective "thought pattern" regarding our futures that contains a big "IF" and that type of stress has never been present within the human condition. Certainly the planet has faced the reality of war before, but in no previous crisis has there been the threat of "no survivors" and the termination of life itself.

Our children are experiencing this tenuous feeling about life far more consciously than many adults; we tend to rationalize our fears or even avoid the subject completely. These young people are now considering their futures with a formula that includes the possibility of nuclear war: "If we can avoid a nuclear exchange, then I'll be able to grow up and have a family and a career."

While within our adult worlds we may go about the business of our lives "as usual," nothing is usual anymore. This fear for survival has penetrated each one of us—the only difference is, perhaps, our degrees of personal awareness. Some of us are more conscious than others of the extreme and critical circumstances in which we now live. For many people, however, the depth of the nuclear crisis remains incomprehensible—situation that is simply not real. Yet, despite the fact that we might prefer to think of this crisis as not actually "real," it has become impossible to be a resident of this planet and exist outside the fear of nuclear attack, even if one never mentions the words "nuclear war." We are breathing the fear into our systems moment by moment, whether or not we are aware of it.

Consider that our sense of security is dependent upon our belief in the strength and competency of our governments to settle international conflicts. Yet, every day we watch the competency level of our governments fluctuate as dramatically as the stock market, all the while knowing—even if that knowing is subliminal—that the underlying issue which is being negotiated in every situation has the potential of igniting a global conflict. Whether the crisis concerns hostages or oil, we observe each crisis wondering "if" it will get out of hand. We have created a world situation in which, given our vast nuclear arsenals, it has become impossible to have an insignificant crisis.

THE ECOLOGICAL FACTOR (Myss)

This fear for survival is equally present as we observe the entire planetary environment deteriorate in massive chunks daily. We no longer measure our destructive capabilities by generation, or even by decade. We now have statistics indicating how much destruction is occurring each day—and where. We know exactly how many species are becoming extinct; we know that our drinking water is becoming more and more contaminated; we know that our air is becoming dangerous to breathe; and we know that raising crops that are both nutritious and untainted by pesticides and other poisons is becoming rare.

These environmental crises have resulted in a growing movement amongst people to protect our world—that is the good news. Simultaneously, however, the deteriorating quality of the environment of this planet has intensified the human fear of being without the basic requirements for life: food, water, air, energy. The fear of shortages—of not having enough—has penetrated into every person's thinking process. True, human beings have always been concerned with survival needs, and in many nations survival needs are anything but new. The difference now, however, is that as a planet we are facing the actual depletion or total contamination of these basic necessities for life. These shortages are no longer related to one's personal finances—they exist because the planet itself is becoming poisoned.

We are now living within a critical time zone for life itself. And, as with the potential of nuclear destruction, no one exists outside the boundaries of this ecological crisis. Whether or not we are conscious of feeling the sting of this fear does not interfere with its ability to affect us.

This crisis is symbolized by the suffering that abounds in Ethiopia, as well as in other nations. In Ethiopia, millions of people are dying of starvation in a nation whose clouds refuse to produce rain, whose fields refuse to bear grain. The Ethiopian situation stands as a warning from Nature itself; the capacity that Nature has to restore a system of balance to the environment cannot accommodate the extent to which we are interfering with our ecology. Nature may be attempting to make a plea on behalf of this earth, through the devastating situation in Ethiopia, that we cease our abusive treatment of life on this planet lest the entire planet suffer.

THE LINK TO AIDS (Myss)

AIDS, like the nuclear crisis and the threatened condition of our ecology, is a global problem. The virus is not contained within the boundaries of any nation but is, in fact, spreading throughout the planet. It is becoming the first full-scale planetary epidemic. Scientific projections warn that AIDS will take the lives of at least 100 million people before any degree of control is established.

The AIDS virus is pernicious; it apparently has been spreading invisibly for possibly a decade or more. Though awareness about AIDS is rapidly increasing, this virus is still capable of spreading unchecked. Carriers often have no awareness or symptoms of infection and transmit the disease unknowingly.

How have the nuclear crisis and our ecological crisis contributed to creating conditions that are ripe for the AIDS epidemic?

Understanding the link which connects AIDS to the nuclear crisis and our ecological situation begins with examining the emotional, psychological and spiritual stresses that contribute to the creation of this disease. Identifying the factors within the creation of disease is the major focus of the work that Norm and I do together; and AIDS, like every disease, requires a specific emotional and psychological climate in which to thrive.

THE CHARACTERISTICS OF AIDS: CASE STUDIES (Myss)

Just as each disease has a specific set of physical characteristics that are the known properties of the illness, so also does each disease have emotional, psychological and spiritual characteristics. Many times these characteristics are not given serious consideration because emotional and psychological strain cannot be quantified in the same manner as a white blood cell count. Nevertheless, these factors of human pain exist as very real and powerful contributors to the condition of disease.

Since 1985, I have worked closely with people who have AIDS. Some of these individuals are homosexual. Others became infected with AIDS through blood transfusions or through sexual contact with partners who are bisexual or prostitutes. The striking similarities that exist among all of these cases are found in the emotional and psychological profiles of these individuals. In spite of backgrounds that vary socially, economically and educationally, the self-images that these individuals hold reveal a common territory of internal pain.

I describe the dominant characteristic among people who develop AIDS as "victim consciousness." In my experience, this characteristic is what I recognize as the core weakness within the personalities of AIDS patients. All of the other emotional and psychological characteristics of such people exist as a result of "victim consciousness."

WHAT IS VICTIM CONSCIOUSNESS? (Myss)

Victim consciousness is a perception of oneself as so completely lacking in personal power that one continually fears being taken advantage of or hurt in some way. This sense of inadequacy is so dominant that the person assumes that he or she will always be at some level of disadvantage in most situations and therefore must always take precautions— sometimes extreme precautions—to protect oneself. "Victim consciousness" means living in the belief that the world is an unfair place and that it is mostly unfair to you.

To some extent, we all know what it is to feel victimized. That is because we all have areas within our lives in which we do not feel adequate, capable or qualified. For some people, relationships are the most threatening of circumstances, and such individuals find it almost impossible to create balanced, loving relationships. For others, achieving financial security seems to be the impossible mountain to climb. Any circumstance in life in which a person feels a lack of personal power can result in the fear of being victimized. When any situation arises that activates our lack of power, it is not uncommon for us to respond by becoming defensive or panicked. These feelings and reactions are typical of victim consciousness.

There is also a form of victim consciousness that is considered normal social behavior. People who live in cities or in high crime rate districts know how many precautions are deemed necessary to protect themselves from being mugged, raped, murdered or burglarized. Consider all of the legal precautions that are deemed necessary in business transactions to avoid being cheated; that is, to compensate for the fact that we assume dishonesty in our transactions rather than honesty. While we think of the elaborate steps people must take to ensure their safety as "normal," recognize that the underlying fear motivating this protective behavior is the fear of becoming someone's victim. In other words, adapting a form of victim consciousness has become necessary for survival in most of our environments. And while none of us finds it comforting to think of ourselves as having a fear of being victimized, *nonetheless, a degree of victim consciousness lives in us all.*

VICTIM CONSCIOUSNESS AND AIDS (Myss)

Victim consciousness is, for the most part, a learned form of behavior in most individuals. It develops in response to negative experiences or to having to adapt to a particularly threatening environment. Considering the violent texture of our present world, it may be impossible to avoid some level of this feeling. Yet, this need not become the major lens through which we see the whole of life. While most of us experience a degree of victim consciousness, most of us would not assess the whole of life as a brutal and unfair experience.

My experience with people who have developed AIDS is that they view life—that is, they view being alive—as a deeply threatening experience. Unlike the previously described forms of victim consciousness, these individuals share a feeling of either having been born "one of life's natural victims," or believing that they began life battling such great odds that they never had a fair chance to make their lives work, even from the beginning. One young man described it to me as "being born already defeated." He added, "I had nothing going for me in this life. I'm gay, I'm broke, I'm frightened and now I have AIDS. Now, not even my family wants anything to do with me." More than any other descriptive phrase, being born "one of life's natural victims" captures the essence of victim consciousness for individuals suffering with AIDS. The common psychological territory that these people share embodies a type or quality of powerlessness that comes from believing that who and what they are is simply not acceptable within our present social environment; for example, being homosexual, a prostitute or a drug addict. If we were to speak of our society in terms of a caste system, the people who have AIDS would be found on the lowest level. Think of this caste system as applying to both social status and to psychological/emotional suffering. The emotional and psychological problems of people who become drug addicts or prostitutes do not usually elicit an empathetic response from the rest of society. Instead of recognizing the overwhelming sense of desperation or powerlessness in these people, we often reduce their problems to "immoral behavior" or "socially unacceptable actions."

Note also that this feeling of powerlessness is not solely associated with economic status, although economics is a major factor. The self-image of being a powerless person exists even among affluent individuals with AIDS. Being "one of life's natural victims" is a self-image that comes from feeling that no matter what you achieve in life, no matter how successful you might become, no matter how loving and sensitive a person you are, nothing you can accomplish will help you to change those things about yourself that are simply not acceptable within the present social environment. It is practically impossible for anyone who suffers with this self-image to feel good about life and safe in this world.

The issue of safety is particularly central to AIDS patients, both physically and emotionally. For many homosexuals, being open about their lifestyles may result in social persecu-

tion, job loss and family stress. "Hiding," so to speak, or living a dual identity develops as a matter of survival. One lives
on the edge of being discovered or found out and conse-
quently harmed or threatened in some way.

What does it mean to feel "threatened?" When we are
threatened—whether that be in a conversation with another
person or in responding to something threatening on the
streets of our cities—our defenses surface as a form of protection. This feeling of fear and the need to protect oneself
trigger certain physiological reactions. Adrenalin, for instance,
begins to run and we initially feel more alert, more energetic
or more nervous. The activity of the immune system also increases when a person feels vulnerable or fears some form
of attack. The immune system, of course, protects the physical
body from the potentially harmful effects of germs, bacteria
and viruses. The immune system also responds to emotional
signals in much the same way as the adrenal system. When
a person is feeling vulnerable, under attack, or "victimized,"
the "emotional immune system" is activated, becoming a protective force field around the body.

Now consider that AIDS is a condition in which the immune system no longer functions. I do not believe it to be
a coincidence that victim consciousness—fear for one's personal safety—characterizes the psychological profiles of AIDS
patients. I believe, in fact, that this state of consciousness—
that of victim—works like a magnet to attract the virus directly
to a person who no longer feels able to protect him- or herself.
Symbolically, I would describe the condition of such people
as one in which the "emotional immune system" has become
exhausted or reached "burn out." This psychological and emotional climate then becomes the culture medium in which the
HIV virus can take hold.

This analysis of the consciousness of AIDS may also provide a degree of insight into the reason that AIDS has emerged in epidemic proportions among only certain social groups—mainly homosexuals, intravenous drug users, Haitians, prostitutes, and certain populations of Africa. The people in these groups are among the most powerless on our planet, and therefore the most vulnerable.

The following case studies are included in order to illustrate further the characteristics of victim consciousness as they have manifested within the lives of these AIDS patients. I share what I have noted as the emotional and psychological issues common to AIDS patients in order to challenge the belief that only homosexuals are capable of developing AIDS. After two years of working with people who have AIDS, I have come to believe that anyone who is manifesting these emotional and psychological characteristics can POTENTIALLY attract AIDS.

I will add that in general, most of the 100 AIDS patients I have worked with would not have described themselves as "victims" prior to their diagnosis of AIDS. Many were aware that their lives were not fulfilling to them, but they would not have listed the reason for their discontentment as rooted in victim consciousness. However, once presented with a description of victim consciousness, a majority of these people found it to be a valid representation of their self image.

CASE STUDIES   *Please note that the names used in these studies have been changed in order to ensure confidentiality.

ALEX

STATISTICS: Born in New York City, 44 years old, actor/model, resident of New York City. Diagnosed with AIDS in January 1984. Died July 1986. The conversations quoted in this booklet were taken directly from our conversations, personal letters or notes taken during our telephone therapy sessions.

Alex grew up in Long Island, New York. He described himself as being painfully shy as a boy and remembered most social interactions as a teenager and a young man as "excruciatingly difficult." In addition to his shyness causing him to be uncomfortable with people, Alex became aware that he was gay at the age of 12. Although he did not know at that time about homosexuality, Alex had a sense that the strong attraction he was feeling to members of the same sex was not acceptable.

Alex did not discuss his awakening to his homosexuality with anyone until he was in his early twenties and living on his own. The "silent decade," as he remembers it, from age 12 to 22, he recalled as "pure hell." "For one thing," said Alex, "I realized somewhere around the age of 15 that girls found me attractive. My father liked the fact that women were attracted to me and so he was always pushing me into social activities, just as he was always pushing me into sports.

"I played football in high school, mainly because I didn't want my parents or anyone else to know that I was gay. I used to work out all the time and keep my body very well developed. This was the irony for me. I would do all these athletics so that no one would think I was gay, and that attracted women to me constantly. The social pressure for me was unbearable. I would start sweating the moment I would leave the house to pick up a date, and all I was able to think about when I was out for an evening with a girl was how to avoid kissing her when I took her home at night.

"By the time I was a college freshman, hiding my gayness became practically impossible. While I was in high school, I had to work at making my mannerisms more masculine. My normal way of expressing myself is much softer than how I forced myself to speak when I was in high school. I decided that as soon as I started college, I would let me be me. Once I actually got to college, I realized that I wasn't looking just to be able to speak a certain way. I wanted to 'come out.' I wanted to be me completely and that meant being gay openly and not having to hide anymore."

Alex completed college with a degree in graphic arts. He moved to Manhattan in 1963 and started to develop his social life as a gay man. For the next 10 years, Alex continued to live a double life because he realized that many of his graphic arts clients would be uncomfortable if they knew he was gay. In his private social life, however, Alex was beginning to enjoy a sense of openness for the first time in his life. And he began to explore the possibility of developing an intimate relationship during this time.

Alex recalled each of his attempts at creating a successful relationship during the 1960's as a "painful effort to have a normal life which was destined for failure."

"Where are the role models for a gay couple relationship? There aren't any, at least there weren't any back then. So, the situation was like this: most of us would have loved to have a close relationship and all that that means in terms of a home, but when you have to keep your life secret from so many people, there's no place where you can even live that is really normal. Being gay means you have to live in the gay part of town, you frequent gay bars and restaurants, you buy your clothes at gay shops. There is nothing normal about that type of living.

"It's impossible to have a long-term intimate relationship in this type of social environment because basically none of us believes it's possible, so why even try. We just get used to quick relationships, some lasting for only two weeks, and a lot of sex."

Two new elements came into Alex's life in 1971 which changed his life more dramatically than he had ever thought possible: 1) bath houses and anonymous sex, and 2) a career in modeling. With the encouragement of several of his friends, Alex decided to try his skill in the modeling industry. He was delightfully overwhelmed with the response. Alex had continued his discipline of physical exercise which he had developed during his high school years so his body was in fine shape. This made him a popular model for outdoor sporting shots. He was also tall and his trim frame meant he could wear clothes particularly well. With minimal effort, Alex became a success as a model in New York.

For the first time in his life, Alex began to feel good about himself. So good, in fact, that he no longer cared to hide the fact that he was gay from anyone, including his clients and his family. He told his family that he was gay and his parents and his brother rejected him. Not unexpectedly, Alex did lose some of his graphics clients, but that was not much of a problem for him since he was earning a comfortable income from his now frequent modeling jobs.

This newfound personal freedom gave Alex the push he needed to begin to visit the bath houses, which had become a popular meeting place within the gay community for anonymous sex. Alex began by going once or twice a week. Within four months, Alex was a daily patron at the bath houses, having as many as 40 or 50 sexual partners each week. The term "sexual partner" is not meant to imply a relationship. Rather, it refers to a person with whom one engages in anonymous sex.

This lifestyle continued until Alex received his diagnosis of AIDS in 1984. There were periods of time during this span of 13 years in which Alex would cease his bath house activities for a week or two, intent on not returning. But inevitably he would return to the cycle of anonymous sex. Like so many other gay men who have shared their personal histories with me, Alex described the cycle of bath house sex as an addiction. Anonymous sex, first of all, became associated with the gay lifestyle in New York and therefore a type of identification process became a part of the addiction. These types of sexual encounters have an element of excitement to them that exists as almost the antithesis to the excitement and passion of a romantic heterosexual relationship.

Alex described himself during these 13 years as "unconscious," never really concerned about anyone but himself. He "let his vanity run his life," and lived solely to satisfy his ego. He recalled that had he stopped and thought about his life—even for an afternoon—he would have realized that he really did not have much of a life. "It's funny how you can see what you want to see. Before I had AIDS, I thought my life was great. I had money, I had sex. I traveled. I thought my apartment in New York was so special. Now I look at it and my apartment feels like a cell to me. When I was healthy, I could come and go as I please. Now, I have to stay here because I am too weak to go anywhere and I'm alone most of the time. I think of all those people out there that I have known in some way, or been with sexually, and I wonder what they would say if they could see me in this condition. You know, most of them don't know I have AIDS...maybe most of them haven't even noticed I'm not around."

ALEX AND THE HEALING PROCESS

Alex was diagnosed with AIDS/pneumocystis in January 1984. Like so many others who learn they have AIDS, Alex did not share his news with anyone, but retreated into the desperate pursuit of trying to heal AIDS alone. The reaction to learning one has AIDS is personally and socially paralyzing. One expects to be shunned from hospitals and other health care facilities unless they have an already established reputation for handling patients with AIDS.

Friends and even family members may have reactions of fear, withdrawing an effective level of emotional support. Because of the stigma of shame and the contagious nature of the disease, individuals seek as much help as they can find while keeping the diagnosis a secret for as long as possible. This was how Alex initially responded to his diagnosis.

His journey began with visits to traditional physicians who were able to help his early outbreaks of fevers as well as the pain and weakness developing in his lungs. Eventually, Alex started to seek alternative healing practices, including the help of a Tibetan physician. He changed to a vegetarian diet and started to treat himself with Tibetan herbs. Simultaneously, Alex began a series of acupuncture treatments.

Alex withdrew from his active social life, and by the summer of 1984 felt directed to pursue personal spiritual matters. His health by this time had regained some strength and Alex began to believe that he would recover from AIDS. He became familiar with the AIDS Action Committee in New York City and started to volunteer for the cause. He felt that he had a great deal to offer other people suffering with AIDS since he was certain that he was on his way back to health.

The late fall of 1984 marked a turning point for Alex. His financial situation started to shift dramatically. Physically, he was no longer able to continue working as a model. Modeling had become Alex's main source of income, and during the years of his modeling career he had discontinued most, if not all, of his vital graphic arts clients. Now he had to force himself to start that career all over again and the prospect of doing that was totally overwhelming. He began to fear being evicted from his apartment, not being able to feed himself, and having nowhere but the streets to live.

These fears pressed heavily on Alex, and by January 1985 he was hospitalized for difficulty with breathing. This was to be the first of several periods of hospitalization which came to terrify Alex. Some of the treatments he endured were so painful for him that even when he recalled them in our conversations, he would shake with emotion.

The panic of AIDS cannot be exaggerated. Since there is so little anyone can do to heal the immune system, anyone offering any hope, any new treatment, any potential for life extension, becomes a beacon of light. Part of the panic exists because of the devastating effects the virus has on the physical body. Death by AIDS is brutal. Part of the panic is also financial. AIDS is expensive. The situation Alex found himself in is the most common amongst AIDS patients: no insurance, no money and yet desperately needing help. Alex experienced several humiliating and frightening instances in which he felt compelled to tell a physician that he was unable to pay for any treatment. In certain situations, he was treated but asked not to return. Yet, his comment to me was that so many of these people turned out to be deeply compassionate.

By August 1985, Alex was in a substantially weakened position. He only had enough strength to be mobile for a few hours each day. He had become dependent upon friends for providing his food each day. He was two months behind in his rent money and terrified that his landlord would evict him, in particular if he learned that Alex had AIDS. In order to survive financially through the fall, Alex had to call his parents. For him, this was almost as difficult as dealing with AIDS. His parents lived 50 miles away from New York City, and yet had not made an effort to see Alex since learning that he was homosexual. His parents sent a small amount of money, as did his brother, along with their regrets that he was ill. Alex was never to see any of his family members again.

During the fall of 1985, Alex started to experience nightmares and anxiety attacks. Many of his dreams took him back to his childhood—times with his brother or his mother. The reality of his family having rejected him yet again reawakened all of his painful childhood and adolescent memories.

The most extraordinary part of the journey with Alex was spiritual. As each of the parts of his life fell away, leaving him more vulnerable, more alone, more frightened, he somehow found more and more faith and strength. In his words, Alex said, "I never knew how precious could be a visit from a friend, or the gift of a meal. And these gifts have become endless for me. They are happening constantly. Every time I get scared—which is pretty often—I just have to remind myself that God is taking care of me."

In one of the many special moments when "God took care of" Alex, Alex received a phone call from a friend in the Los Angeles area suggesting that Alex move to the west coast. Alex wanted to jump at the opportunity not to have to spend a depressing winter in New York City, and yet Alex was aware that this friend did not know how ill he had become. Alex shared with this friend that he had AIDS and—ironically—this friend had become an AIDS counselor and insisted at that point that Alex move west into a supportive group of people. This friend also provided the money for transportation and accommodations.

Alex moved west shortly before Christmas 1985. By spring, he required private nurses, paid for by this community of people in the Los Angeles area. In a letter to me in the early summer shortly before Alex died, he wrote, "I wish to let go of all my negative belief systems and move forward. I wish to know my path and God's will for me. I wish to be an inspiration for others and be a part of the healing of this planet."

ANNE

STATISTICS: Born in Chicago, 56 years old, wife, mother of three, lifetime resident of Chicago. Diagnosed with AIDS August 1984. Died March 1986. Cases of women with AIDS are predominantly associated with prostitutes. Anne developed AIDS as a result of a blood transfusion. Her story is significant because, unlike prostitutes whose identification with victim consciousness is obvious, Anne's psychological/ emotional profile is far more typical of the subtle way victim consciousness can penetrate our lives.

Anne was the "perfect" wife, mother, neighbor and friend. Everyone loved her. She had a social life that was filled with family, friends and community. From all appearances, Anne had a lovely life, and was completely content with her children and her husband.

Emotionally, however, Anne was completely dependent upon her husband. She enjoyed running the household and taking care of her husband and children, but Anne relied on her husband for financial support and for any decision that had to do with matters outside the home.

In the spring of 1983, Anne's world began to unravel. Her husband was diagnosed with rapidly spreading cancer. Three months later, he died, leaving Anne—at age 53—on her own for the first time in her life. Anne fell into despair not only at the death of her husband, but also at the prospect of having to take care of herself, make her own decisions, and handle her own finances. She believed, as her husband had encouraged her to believe, that she was incapable of taking on these responsibilities despite the assistance that was offered to her by her children.

For Anne, picking up the pieces of her life following the death of her husband seemed impossible. She saw herself as completely vulnerable and unable to protect herself without her husband. He had assured her that he would "always be there" to care for her. Much of the fear that poured out of Anne during this time reflected her inability to consider her life without her husband, much less prepare herself in any way to take care of herself. Now, without him, she saw the world as hostile and overwhelming; she was a woman waiting to be taken advantage of, to be victimized.

Anne became more and more emotionally withdrawn and eventually developed bleeding ulcers from the stress of her situation. In April 1984, hospitalization was required in order to treat the blood loss from her ulcerated stomach. During this time, Anne received six blood transfusions and became infected with the AIDS virus.

By fall 1984, Anne developed a weakness in her lungs. She was hospitalized for pneumonia and in the course of trying to identify the virus in her system, the HIV virus was discovered and her diagnosis changed to pneumocystis.

Anne's encounter with AIDS was particularly tragic since she was totally unfamiliar with the disease. She was unaware of both the fear that surrounds the virus and its association with homosexuality and, therefore, she was unprepared for the experiences she encountered. Since Anne's diagnosis occurred prior to the recent outpouring of educational material and empathetic concern, the hospital staff responded with more fear than compassion. She was immediately isolated. Anne fell victim to much of the fear felt by the hospital staff. Nurses were either uncomfortable treating her or refused any contact with her at all. Orderlies refused to deliver her meals, often leaving them on the floor outside the door to her room. She recalled noticing people staring at her or walking out of their way to avoid the possibility of even bumping into her. The humiliation was devastating for Anne.

Anne returned home as soon as she was able and her children provided much of her care until her death in March 1986. Following her husband's death, Anne assumed entirely the emotional and psychological profile of a powerless human being. Unable to break free of her belief that, without her husband, life would victimize her, she manifested these deepest fears in the last year and a half of her life.

JACK

STATISTICS: Born in New York City, 36 years old, married, salesman for a major corporation, resident of New York City. Diagnosed with AIDS June 1984. Died November 1985.

In many ways, Jack exemplified the personality and ambitions associated with the young corporate executive. He was shrewd in the ways of business and knew just how to invest his capital in commercial real estate in order to make enormous profits in short time spans. He saw himself as one of those lucky people who would retire at age 49 with several million dollars in the bank and years to enjoy the good life.

Socially, Jack was not as skilled as he was in terms of finance. His priorities were clearly money and power, with very little appreciation for the people within his life. Jack was impatient and hot tempered, often becoming irrational over insignificant problems. Despite his outbursts of temper, he rarely apologized for his actions. He considered these patterns of behavior to be appropriate to an ambitious man.

Essentially, Jack's philosophy about life was "get them before they get you." He was a person totally controlled by his fears, though, from his perspective, he had everything under control. He was continually plagued with anxiety attacks about other people getting ahead of him or making better deals.

Jack married when he was 29. He partnered with a quiet, supportive woman who seemed to want a fairly traditional relationship. They had decided to put off starting a family until Jack felt that he had established a sound financial foundation for them. As Jack's wife later realized, Jack's feeling of "financial security" always seemed to be one more deal away.

When Jack felt successful and good about himself, he was charming and more generous. He believed in celebrating his financial milestones, and sometimes part of his personal celebration included an evening with a prostitute.

During the spring of 1984, Jack noticed a shift in his health. He started to experience a loss of energy, night sweats and an aching sensation in his joints. He attributed this condition to stress. In May, Jack spotted five or six purple lesions on his arms and one on his neck.

Jack received a diagnosis of AIDS/Kaposi sarcoma in June 1984. In spite of the disclosure that he had become infected through sexual activity with a prostitute, Jack's wife remained with him throughout the course of his illness.

Perhaps the most extraordinary element of Jack's life was that his diagnosis of AIDS drew much support from the friends and family members around him. Even though he had lived a rather self-centered life, Jack was loved almost in spite of himself. Yet, Jack focused only on his anger that he had AIDS. His wife said that he would spend hours at a time repeating to himself, "I don't deserve this."

Jack's attitude about his physical circumstance no doubt assisted the rapid spread of the disease. Attempts to encourage Jack to work with alternative methods of healing, nutrition or visualization were mostly in vain. At one point, I shared the characteristics of victim consciousness with Jack, hoping that he would see a value in working to heal his self-image. He exploded: "Why should I try to help myself? I shouldn't have this god...n disease in the first place. I'm not one of them [homosexual] and I'm no f.....g victim."

Jack died in November 1985, bitter and angry, believing that his suffering was a part of a cruel joke that was perpetrated by a malevolent God.

COMMENTARY (Myss)

These three people represent some of the many faces and the many forms of victim consciousness. Sometimes the characteristics are obvious, as they were with Alex and Jack. Sometimes, as with Anne, they are hidden, absorbed by the larger scheme of a person's life.

Without exception, every person with AIDS that I have encountered has characteristics of victim consciousness that are dominant in his or her life. It is these characteristics, I now believe, that act as a magnet which attracts the HIV virus to such an individual through the circumstances that are present in that person's life. We may think that it is an "accident," for instance, that Anne received a blood transfusion that contained the AIDS virus; yet, such an occurrence is not an "accident" from the point of view that recognizes the basic "law of attraction" (i.e., like attracts like) that operates within each person's life. Anne's emotional/psychological "magnetic field" influenced the process of selecting the blood transfusions for her. This may sound unlikely, yet consider that within the many areas of our lives, we are very accepting of the activity of the law of attraction. We accept the principles that "money attracts money," "power attracts power," "greed attracts greed." Is this process of attraction, in essence, any different?

Why is the HIV virus seemingly attracted to individuals who share this emotional and psychological profile? The answer to that question requires that we bring into focus the conditions of stress that are present on our earth.

THE PLANETARY CONNECTION:
THE SYMBOLIC MESSAGE OF AIDS (Myss)

Why AIDS now? Certainly, we can produce physical reasons for the spread of the AIDS virus; we are, for example, more mobile and sexually open than ever before and these factors are major contributors toward this disease becoming a planetary epidemic. Physical factors, however, do not explain why the virus has come into the world at this particular "time period." What are the elements present in our world that make it possible for AIDS to exist? Are we meant to learn something from this epidemic? Does this disease hold a symbolic message?

These questions bring us back to examining the factors of stress that are present in our world—the potentials of a nuclear devastation and massive ecological disasters—and to a consideration of how these factors relate not only to victim consciousness but also to the planet itself.

We are unaccustomed to thinking about planet Earth as having "consciousness." Most of us have never considered that the earth exists as a form of life that is independent of the human experience and that, as a form of life, the earth has spirit and intelligence. This is a perception that is not novel to certain spiritual traditions, but many individuals have never given such mystical perceptions scientific or medical credibility, much less serious environmental concern.

Yet, keep in mind that AIDS thrives upon and is drawn to victim consciousness. The threat of nuclear devastation has made us all potential victims — including the earth itself. Not only do we now hold each other "nuclearly hostage," we are holding the earth nuclearly hostage as well, because the earth will not survive a nuclear war any better than we will.

Is it possible that the earth is responding to this prolonged threat to its own survival? Indeed, is it possible that the reason that the AIDS epidemic has exploded upon us now is that the earth itself has AIDS — the result, as in the case of human beings, of emotional, psychological and physical stresses having reached a breaking point? The earth itself is now a victim of the same stresses that threaten human survival.

AIDS results in two major physical illnesses: pneumocystis, which is a serious lung infection, and Kaposi sarcoma, which is the development of cancerous lesions beneath the skin. Imagine the earth as if it were a human being. Now consider the massive destruction of the rain forests of South America and the destruction of the forests of North America and Europe from acid rain. These forests are the lungs of the earth and they are rapidly becoming unable to produce oxygen. Further, the air over every major city of the earth is polluted and this pollution is spreading to even less populated regions. The earth has developed "pneumocystis."

Then look at the lesions that are created within the earth by nuclear explosions underground and the lesions that are created through abuse of the land. These destructive lesions are physically analogous to Kaposi sarcoma—cancerous lesions located beneath the surface of the human body. The earth has "Kaposi sarcoma."

The ionosphere of the earth—that protective atmospheric womb in which the earth resides—symbolically represents the earth's immune system. Recently, a hole has been found in the ionosphere above the South Pole. Scientists do not know the extent of the effect(s) that this hole will have upon the earth, but they are critically concerned.

It may be that the earth, a consciousness that is as alive and vital as we are, is suffering from "AIDS" as a result of the same oppressing victim consciousness that is threatening all of humanity. In a desperate attempt to purge humankind of the need to prey on life, AIDS has manifested through our collective consciousness as an opportunity to release our human pattern of the need to victimize life—a pattern of behavior which can no longer exist on a planet that has come into the nuclear age. Perhaps it is for this reason that the groups of people who are presently most susceptible to AIDS exhibit in common a profile of acute victim consciousness: they embody, at the human level, the identical stresses of the earth, and therefore they appropriately carry the message that the victimization of any form of life must cease lest the planet become uninhabitable either through nuclear devastation or ecological disasters.

CHILDREN AND AIDS (Myss)

A growing number of infants are being born with AIDS as a result of their mothers having been infected with the virus. Some of these infants have been left to the care of hospital personnel. Other children have contracted the virus as a result of blood transfusions. Can the explanation of "victim consciousness" be applied to children? Perhaps not as obviously; yet, there is a connecting link.

Children differ from adults in terms of their levels of maturity—not in terms of the biological or emotional systems. Nevertheless they are as susceptible to the stress factors we feel as adults, though they are limited in their abilities to express this. "Victim consciousness" is a characteristic of the human condition, like germs and bacteria. As such, every human being who is born into the earth's atmosphere becomes immersed in all the conditions of the earth's atmosphere. Part of this immersion includes exposure to the psychological and emotional stresses that form the configuration of life. If a child is born into a place where the air is thickly polluted, then his or her lungs will become contaminated, regardless of the loving attention given to this child from the parents. Pollution is a stress factor of the earth's condition.

It is difficult for many of us to grapple with the reality of children and illness. We hold in our minds a belief that childhood is or should be a time of innocence and carefree enchantments. What is more often the case, however, is that the pressure and stresses that affect our lives as adults spill over into the worlds of our children. They are deeply influenced by the difficulties of life. Children die in wars. Children starve. Children are molested. Children are abused and neglected. Children become addicted to drugs and alcohol. These sufferings are not infrequent. In fact, they are all too common. And they are all indications that the innocence we associate with childhood is an inaccurate perception that prevents us from appreciating the intelligence and sensitivities of our young people.

Now, many of our children are aware of the nuclear crisis. The late Samantha Smith, a youngster from Maine, became an international figure because of a letter she wrote to Soviet Premier Mikail Gorbachev on behalf of peace. Were she unaware of the possibility of nuclear war, she might never have been inspired to write such a message to the Soviet Union. Children are rapidly growing in awareness that the planet which is presently facing the possibility of complete destruction, is also their home.

As we seek to expand our understanding of disease—all diseases, not just AIDS—we must consider including children as equal to adults in their capacity to become overwhelmed by the psychological and emotional stresses that fill the atmosphere of the world in which they live.

PART II:

THE HEALING OF AIDS

The Healing of AIDS

Caroline M. Myss, M.A.

CAN AIDS BE HEALED?

My personal belief is that any disease can be healed. By this, I do not mean surgically removed or drugged into remission, but completely healed. The question, more authentically, is not can AIDS—or for that matter any disease—be healed, but what are the requirements which must be met in order for healing to occur?

If a person believes disease to be a condition which exists only within the "physical" body, then for that person the requirements for healing will center primarily on responding to the needs of the physical body. Medicine, surgery and more traditional approaches to assist the recovery of health will be the only considerations.

If, however, disease is recognized as a condition that is created through stress in the emotional, psychological and spiritual areas of a person's life, then the requirements for healing must include attention to these factors. My experience has been that complete healing occurs only when the underlying emotional, psychological and spiritual stresses are treated as equal contributing elements to disease. With AIDS, these stresses relate directly to victim consciousness. The healing of AIDS requires the healing of victim consciousness. Treatment of the physical body alone will not result in healing this disease. The confidence with which I assume this position comes from having been a part of one young man's successful healing of AIDS and other success stories in progress.

THE MIRACLE OF PETER (Myss)

I became involved with AIDS in March 1985 when a close friend asked me to do a clairvoyant health evaluation on his son. Bob, a highly successful mid-western businessman, had received an intuitive feeling on this particular Saturday morning in March, that something was wrong with his son.

I had never met Peter and, until this situation, Peter had not heard of me. Peter was a graduate student living on the west coast. When Bob called early on this Saturday morning, I told him that I would be glad to examine his son's energy but that I needed Peter's permission. Within minutes, Bob had called his son, secured permission and called me back at my home in New Hampshire. I told Bob that I would look into his son's energy and speak with him later that day.

As soon as I focused on Peter's name, I clairvoyantly sensed the presence of a disease that seemed familiar to me and yet I could not quite identify it. My initial impression was leukemia but as soon as I had that thought, I knew that I was mistaken. Suddenly, I received an intuitive impression: this is the vibration of AIDS. I knew nothing about AIDS at the time since the disease was not as well known in the spring of 1985 as it is now. What I did know was that I needed to reach Peter immediately, despite the fact that I was not sure what I was going to say to him since I had no idea what help I could be to someone who had an illness that I knew nothing about.

I was able to reach Peter early that Saturday afternoon. I remember saying to him that I was a friend of his father's and did clairvoyant health evaluations, and I remember so clearly his nervous voice on the other end of the phone. For some reason, he immediately trusted me—this stranger's voice on a phone call from New Hampshire. His vulnerability and trust touched me so deeply that for a moment, I lost my own clear intent in terms of what I wanted to say to him.

I began to stutter as I attempted to describe what I did and how I worked. I thought this background would be necessary in order to establish a level of credibility with Peter. Finally, I said, "I've looked into your energy field, your white bloodcell count is way off, and your energy is weakened and...Peter, you have AIDS."

There was a brief, silent pause, and then Peter said, "I just got back my test results for AIDS. I tested positive. Jesus, Caroline, I'm so scared. What am I going to do?" He then shared with me all of the symptoms that he was experiencing: night-sweats, chest weakness and painfulness around the joints.

For Peter, the most intimidating problem centered around his father. Peter was 22 and had yet to tell either of his parents that he was homosexual. He feared the disappointment that he would see in their faces and the rejection that he would experience. This situation made it impossible for Peter to keep his secret any longer.

Peter asked me if I was going to disclose his AIDS diagnosis to his father. I told him that I would not do that, but I also felt that I had to tell Bob that a physical problem had developed. How Peter intended to handle the matter was up to him. My recommendation was that he tell his father everything.

Later that afternoon, I spoke with Bob, telling him that Peter had developed an illness and that disclosure of the details rested with Peter. By Saturday evening, Peter was on a plane headed home to speak with his father. For Bob, the waiting was nerve wracking. He called me (while Peter was en route home) to tell me that he already knew that Peter's problem was too much academic pressure. I told him that was not the case and although I wished I could speak openly, I could not until Peter arrived home.

Twenty minutes later, my phone rang again. This time, Bob said, "I've been thinking of the most horrible thing in the world. And if my son walked in here and said, 'Dad, I'm gay and I have AIDS,' I'd still love him." I held my breath for a moment, wondering what response to give. Then I said, "I hope to God you mean that, Bob, because that is exactly what you are going to hear."

I did not hear from Bob or Peter until the next morning when Bob phoned me to tell me that he and his son were flying out to New Hampshire to meet with me in person. By noon on that Sunday, they had arrived. I met them at the airport. Both men had been up most of the night and their emotional exhaustion showed.

We discussed the meaning of a holistic approach to health and the significance of healing emotional memories. The love that these two men had for each other was deeply obvious. And both of them used this diagnosis of AIDS as an opportunity to share that love as openly as they could. The years of fear stored up in Peter began to disintegrate, replaced by the powerful force of unconditional love.

I then shared with Peter instructions that I had received intuitively to assist the healing of AIDS. These instructions included dietary regulations, vitamin intake, as well as meditation and visualization procedures. (These instructions are discussed in this book in *Part II: The Healing of AIDS*). Part of the instructions included speaking openly with his mother and sister about his homosexuality in order that he could establish clear and open relationships with them. Peter needed to learn to love and to accept who he was, just the way he was, with or without the support of the outside world. The instructions covered a period of six weeks. Peter agreed to follow the program, beginning that day.

Six weeks later, in May 1985, Peter had another blood test. This time he tested negative. In 1986, Peter had another blood test and again, tested negative. In 1987, yet again, Peter tested negative. His health has remained vital since 1985. Peter continues to follow most of the recommended practices that he started in May 1985.

How did Peter heal himself? What part of his personal experience could he share that would be of value to others? The following material is taken directly from a conversation that I had with Peter during the writing of this book. I shared with him my perception that victim consciousness seems to be the common thread amongst people who develop AIDS, and I asked him if he had thought of himself as a victim prior to his diagnosis.

"Absolutely. I felt completely like a victim. I was attached to a sense of powerlessness and even though I saw that I was a victim, I felt that I couldn't change one thing about my circumstance.

"As I was growing up, during my grade school years, for instance, I knew I was different. I wasn't sure how but I knew it was bad. And even though no one told me I was gay, children can perceive the 'consciousness of society,' so to speak, and I can always remember having a sense that there was something wrong with me according to the way society believed.

"When I think of my childhood, the image comes to mind of my being alone in my room, always in the dark with the curtains drawn. Everyone else was outside in the backyard having a bar-b-que and no one came to get me because I was the one who was different. I always saw myself as living in darkness.

"The sad part is even when I grew older and started to form healthy gay relationships, my negative self-image didn't change. I think that many of these relationships were not really very healthy because when we got together, what we shared was the pain. There was nothing really positive or nurturing about these relationships. We just got together to commiserate and I think that characterizes a number of gay relationships. I also think that this is part of the reason that sex between gays is often-times unhealthy because so many gays aren't coming from a resurrected position.

"I think that the one thing that all gay people have in common is fear, and by far the majority of gays are slaves to victim consciousness. We all have fears which have come from experiences of telling family members we're gay, or friends, or wondering what will happen if or when your employer finds out. And based on how you handle these experiences, they will either drive you further into a dead spiritual body, or you will learn to use them as a tool for spiritual growth."

I asked Peter to share why he thought he was able to heal himself.

"I was immediately anointed. After finding out that I had AIDS, I was absolutely surrounded with love. I know that I was unable to pray or meditate in the beginning, but others, like my dad and you, did it for me until I was strong enough to meditate for myself. I think that it was crucial that when I was introduced to my healing process, I wasn't alone. I knew I wasn't doing all that had to be done alone.

"And, I knew that I had a choice about my life and whether or not I wanted to live. I had this strong sense that my life wasn't meant to end at this point. I think I could have died, but the opportunity to choose to live was given to me and fortunately, I had the tools and people around me to help me do it. Also, even BEFORE I had AIDS, I wasn't dead. I still believed in life."

What role did spirituality play in Peter's life, before his diagnosis, during his healing, and what role does it play now?

"Before I was ill, I didn't have any sense of spirituality. I had religion. I practiced a form with no belief in its substance. As a result of being ill, I was able to connect the substance to the form.

"I know I could not have healed without a spiritual connection. That's very clear to me. Understanding what spiritual cleansing means, for instance, allowed me to cure myself of all my deep problems that I had created as a result of being homosexual, such as lying, general dishonesty about my life and who I was, and all the guilt that goes with that way of life. After my healing, spirituality was no longer something I read about. It's what I am and what and how I live."

ONE WHITE CROW (Shealy)

I have met Peter's father and sister and knew of his apparent miraculous healing. In writing this book, I asked if Peter would talk with me. A personal phone call from him confirmed the facts that Caroline has presented. His "positive" blood test was obtained with a pseudonym. He was ill, losing weight and had generalized lymphadenopathy. Beyond any reasonable doubt, Peter had AIDS or advanced ARC. His later negative blood tests, beginning remarkably soon after he began Caroline's recommendations, suggest a truly miraculous recovery. If there is one White Crow, then White Crows must be possible. Interestingly, in 1986, Peter "slipped" in his program and in June 1986 his serum globulin, one indication of immune functions, was below normal, and he had 12% "atypical lymphs," suggesting a viral "fight" going on. By March 1987, these blood tests were also normal. His T4/T8 cell ratio is now essentially normal and he has a negative AIDS antibody test. If there is one person who can recover from the AIDS infections, then others may be able to do the same.

PHYSICAL FACTORS THAT AFFECT IMMUNITY (Shealy)

1. NATURAL IMMUNITY

At birth, most infants are immune to many potentially serious infections, such as poliomyelitis and diphtheria, because of a passive immunity that is acquired from the mother's blood. This advantage is lost by 3 to 6 months of age. Passive immunity is specific: that is, it does not include immunity to all infections, e.g. colds and flu, to which adults have limited immunity and young babies are susceptible.

Additional passive immunity is passed to the baby who nurses. In fact, most mammalian babies cannot survive without colostrum, the mother's antibody-rich first milk. The antibody proteins provide immunity to specific infections. Prior to this century, a majority of individuals died in infancy or childhood; it was the weakest who did not survive.

Evidence suggests that culture-wide influences are cumulative in conveying immunity over a period of many generations to infections that are not indigenous (common to a given population). For instance, Europeans brought both measles and syphilis with them to the New World, diseases to which they had developed some measure of resistance. The Native American populations, however, were devastated by this invasion, having had no previous exposure to these diseases and hence no acquired immunity to them. Infections of these kinds may be conveyed by a wide variety of hosts such as people, insects and animals. Communities typically acquire immunity through subclinical infection (few or no symptoms) or genetic modification. The former process may

occur over days or weeks, while the latter may require centuries. In either situation the most vigorous members of the
exposed community are most likely to survive.

2. VACCINE IMMUNITY

Immunity to infections may be acquired by immunization,
the administration of a vaccine. Vaccines consist of a killed
or a weakened culture of bacteria or viruses of a specific type;
polio, measles, diphtheria, whooping cough, smallpox,
typhoid, tetanus and hepatitis B are examples of diseases in
which vaccination can assist in achieving immunity in the
previously unexposed person.

Successful recovery from infections also may convey vary-
ing degrees of immunity. That is, immunity from exposure
ranges from none at all through various periods of temporary
immunity to permanent immunity. Individuals who have once
had shingles, or even chicken pox (a related virus), very rarely
have a recurrence caused by the shingles virus.

3. TRACKS OF INFECTION

Every microorganism has its preferred way of spreading
within the individual where it resides, and from person to person. For example, colds and flu are transmitted through the
respiratory tract into inhaled air and via hand contact. Cholera,
typhoid and other intestinal tract infections are generally
transmitted by contaminated water and other fluids. Hepatitis
and typhoid may be spread through contaminated food. AIDS,
hepatitis, malaria and encephalitis are among the many
diseases that can be transmitted through blood, perhaps by
contaminated hypodermic needles or an insect bite (if the
bacteria or virus can live in the insect, which does not always
happen).

AIDS, venereal herpes, gonorrhea, syphilis and chlamydia are among the numerous diseases that can be sexually transmitted; they are then known as venereal diseases.

In discussing disease transmission, researchers use terms such as HOST, the individual that harbors the disease; and VECTOR, the individual (person, animal or insect) that spreads the disease. These may be the same or they may be different. In rabies, for example, a dog may have contracted rabies from a local skunk, harbor the disease, and yet look healthy until the virus reproduces to the point of making the dog ill. Depending on the virus or bacteria involved, this incubation period may take days, weeks and even years.

In AIDS, for instance, the incubation period may be as long as 10 years or more in some individuals.

4. NUTRITION

Quite simply, what we eat determines how well we function, how healthy we are. If we live on a "high octane" diet, full of fresh vegetables, rice and other wholesome grains, light on fats and adequate in proteins, the body machine tends to operate efficiently. Vitamins and minerals enhance the immune system. Obviously, healthy nutrition cannot overcome serious lapses in the other areas of our lives; however, a balanced nutritional program is an essential part of one's overall health regime.

5. ENVIRONMENTAL FACTORS

Environmental factors that affect our health and our immunity may be classified as follows:

SEASONAL CHANGES

Seasonal changes and the differences that are inherent in the seasons challenge or coddle the immune system. Colds and flu, for example, occur rarely in summer; they are typically fall, winter and early spring diseases (also the time of year when people tend to congregate in heated buildings, rather than outside in fresh air).

NATURAL LIGHT

Natural light significantly enhances immunity. In an office-bound society, few people get adequate natural light.

POLLUTION

Much of the "fresh" air we breathe isn't; in fact, in industrial areas, the air breathed daily may be the equivalent of smoking one or more packs of cigarettes! Cigarette smokers not only pollute their own bodies, but those of anyone who inhales their smoke. The immune system is challenged daily and may be severely weakened by exposure to toxins in the air, water, food and even clothing.

6. ANTIBIOTIC THERAPY

Antibiotics are wonder drugs when they work, and often they do, but their limitations are often overlooked. Meningitis, ear infections, syphilis, gonorrhea, typhoid, tularemia, malaria, tuberculosis, strep throat, scarlet fever and most pneumonia may respond dramatically to antibiotic therapy. On the other hand, the organisms that cause these diseases can change sufficiently during reproduction so that they become resistant to antibiotics. Gonorrhea is an example. Antibiotics may have annoying, even dangerous side-effects and complications: rashes, kidney and liver failure, destruction of the blood-making system, allergic reactions such as shock. The recent experimental drug, AZT, for treatment of AIDS, for example, causes severe anemia. Patients require blood transfusions every two weeks. Finally, while antibiotics may destroy the offending organism, the body, in its weakened state from combatting infection, may fall prey to another "bug" that has been waiting in the wings for the opportunity to invade.

PHYSIOLOGY OF THE IMMUNE SYSTEM AND ITS RELATIONSHIP TO AIDS (Shealy)

Scientists are only now beginning to unravel the secrets of the body's remarkable immune system. Briefly, this is what we know today:

Our bodies are composed of trillions of cells. Organs such as our lungs, heart, liver and brain are collections of highly specialized cells. A cell measures only a few microns in diameter and is composed of two exquisitely organized parts: the fatty cell membrane, or outer wall, and the central nucleus. The cell membrane surrounds the cell nucleus and contains cytoplasm, a semi-liquid gelatinous substance. Cytoplasm is rich in chemical molecules which produce energy as well as hormones, enzymes and other substances.

Vitamins and minerals are some of the elements vital to the proper functioning of this metabolic process. The cell nucleus lies in or near the center of the cell. Nearly spherical, it contains genes which are linked together, bead-like, to form chromosomes. Human cells each have 46 chromosomes; each chromosome contains approximately 50,000 genes. Genes determine the way in which each cell's cytoplasm operates. Most viruses, including the AIDS HTLV-III (Human T-Lymphtrophic Virus type III, more recently called HIV or Human Immunodeficiency Virus), invade the cell nucleus and alter chemical messages sent from the nucleus to the cytoplasm.

The immune system—part of the blood cell production mechanism—strives to keep our body cells healthy. The highly specialized cells of our immune system may even attack and destroy invading, harmful viruses, bacteria and other damaging organisms, even out-of-control cancer cells. Our bodies are threatened by potentially injurious invaders at all times. In fact, many of them may reside and reproduce harmlessly within us, threatening us only when our immunity is weakened by factors such as an unhealthy lifestyle or accumulated stress or a calamitous event that puts us seriously out of balance. Specifically, what are some of these agents of disaster?

Other than harmful or pathogenic viruses, some of the things that can wreak havoc on the body are bacteria and fungi; parasites such as those which cause malaria, worms, plant material and food. Sometimes lethal, or at least damaging, to the immune system are synthetic chemicals, such as gasoline, diesel fuel, various herbicides, insecticides and other pesticides. All of these agents may be well tolerated by some people while devastating to others.

For example, poison ivy is the kind of irritant that swings from being harmless for some to being disabling for others. Some agents are exceedingly choosy in their targets even within the same potential victim. The skin, for instance, may be impervious to an organism which attacks a person through a bloodstream; sexually transmitted diseases commonly behave in this fashion, either attacking mucous membrane or entering the bloodstream through small tears in the rectum, anus and intestine, the vagina and adjacent female organs, the urethra, the nose and the mouth. The remarkable immune system is alerted to the foreign nature of these invaders, which are called antigens, and reacts to neutralize or destroy them. Immune system activity requires energy to meet an emergency. If the person is already in a weakened condition for whatever reason, the immune system's efficacy is impaired. Once an antigen is identified, macrophages, a type of white blood cell, engulf the antigen. The ensuing battle to destroy the invader outclasses in its intricacy and elegance even the most remarkable military maneuvers.

Now the T-cell lymphocytes are aroused. Detecting the surface antigen, they secrete chemical alerters, lymphokines, which alert other lymphocytes, B-cells. B-cells manufacture antibodies, specific proteins and globulins, which adhere to the specific antigen and coat it. Such coated antigens attract phagocytes (also called polymorphonuclear cells), the clean-up crew of white blood cells. Phagocytes devour the coated antigens.

The B-cells, once activated to produce antibodies, become plasma cells which make only one specific antibody. Plasma cells, however, can produce up to 500 "clones" of each cell per day; each plasma cell can produce up to 2,000 antibody molecules per second. The B-cells and their activated "off-spring" compose the humoral immune system (named for the antibody "humor" they release into the blood stream). The B-cells and plasma cells tend to lose their "memory" for most antigens over time (from weeks to years); thus, immunity fades or disappears.

The system is elegantly devised to protect the body. As we understand how it works and its importance to our health and survival, we can appreciate the steps needed to protect and heal the immune system. The T-cells, macrophages and phagocytes are the physical components of the immune system: the "cellular immune system."

Another important component of the cellular immune system is the Natural Killer cell, a lymphocyte, which destroys cancer cells. Macrophages may also devour and "digest" cancer cells. Almost 25% of the body's 100 trillion cells are involved in the immune system. Lymphocytes, macrophages and red blood cells are produced in the bone marrow; over 60 million white blood cells are produced each hour of life.

The B-cells travel from the bone marrow through the bloodstream to lymph nodes and the spleen where they nest to be bathed by lymph flowing through the nodes and the spleen. When the B-cells detect an antigen, they begin their rapid reproduction. The lymph nodes enlarge to handle the increased work load. The acellular lymph circulation is a mostly acellular milky fluid; it flows through a network separate from but as diffusely widespread as the blood circulation.

T-cells leave their bone marrow womb and travel to the thymus gland. This lies at the top, front and center of the chest behind the sternum (breastbone). Thymus hormones nurture the T-cells to mature into several types of alerters. These include the T-4 helper, or inducer, cells (also called T-helper or T4 cells) which release a call-to-action type hormone; this alerts the B-cells.

The HIV virus, AIDS, invades the cell nucleus of the T-4 cells and shuts off the alarm system, not only to the AIDS antigen, but to many other antigens as well. The AIDS virus assumes control of the most important part of the immune defense system, the "alarm." A single virus can produce over 20,000 new viruses per day. Each virus can destroy a T-4 cell and then move on to invade other cells.

Actually, the viruses of many diseases, including measles, herpes, rabies, small pox, mononucleosis (Epstein-Barr virus) and cytomegalovirus damage T-4 cells. In fact, some non-viral illnesses such as lupus erythematosus also lead to decreased T-cell production. When T-cell production is decreased, the B-cells respond inadequately to produce the required antibodies. The body's defenses are thus weakened. At this point, the body becomes susceptible to other infections and cancer.

Fortunately, a number of therapies increase T-cell production, including castor oil packs and herbs such as Echinacea and Ligusticum. Yet, prevention of disease through continued strengthening of the immune system is by far the safest course.

Critical factors in maintaining the health or integrity of the immune system are protein, vitamins, minerals and essential fatty acids (i.e., nutrition) and an awareness of the impact of stress on the body. Stress includes the TOTAL chemical, physical and emotional pressure upon an individual. Hans Selye, the great stress research scientist, demonstrated many years ago that stress producers include (but are not limited to):

CHEMICAL	PHYSICAL	EMOTIONAL
nicotine	obesity	fear
caffeine	inactivity	guilt
alcohol	temperature	anger
sugar	extremes	depression
high fat intake	accidents	anxiety

All mental anguish, especially fear and depression, is a stress on the body. In fact, depression may be a more serious stress overload for the body than a chemical strain. Depression tends to be constant, while chemical stresses tend to be intermittent and temporary.

The stress reaction creates a vicious cycle.

As a result, in prolonged stress:
—the thymus shrinks
—cortisone production remains high
—blood sugar is high (feeds germs)
—thyroid function slows
—sex hormone production decreases
—appetite decreases
—white blood cells decrease
—T-8 suppressor cells decrease

TRANSMISSION OF AIDS (Shealy)

AIDS is known unequivocally to be transmitted from one person to another through blood and semen. Although any body fluid might contain the virus (e.g., saliva, feces, tears, sweat, vaginal fluids) other factors are perhaps more important.

In Africa, mosquitoes, cockroaches, antlions, tsetse flies and other insects are infected with the virus.

Despite widely reported "fragility" of the AIDS virus, it has been found to survive 15 days at room temperature, and it lives for at least 10 days in a "dried" state.

Major medical reasons that homosexuals have manifested AIDS more commonly than heterosexuals are:

1. Oral ingestion of semen

2. Anal intercourse which often leads to bleeding as well as introduction of semen. Homosexuals also have a higher incidence of giardiasis, an intestinal parasite which also weakens the immune system.

3. Successive relationships, as opposed to monogamous relationships, which may involve more than 100 different partners a year.

Hepatitis B, anemia, poor nutrition, lack of sleep and other "stress" factors such as the use of Quaalude(s) have all been correlated with susceptibility to AIDS. Venereal herpes and candida (yeast) infections, often present in AIDS patients, are also indications of a weakened immune system. Blood transfusions and contaminated needles are an obvious source of AIDS transmission. Thus the intravenous drug addict is another common "victim" of AIDS. Infants may be born with AIDS transmitted via the mother's blood.

Hemophiliacs are innocent victims as well, dependent as they often are on blood transfusions.

Bisexually-oriented individuals, even more common than those who are homosexual, are an inevitable host for the transmission of AIDS to the heterosexual population. AIDS is becoming increasingly prevalent among heterosexuals; in fact, in Africa, AIDS is NOT considered a homosexual problem.

PREVENTIVE MEASURES (Shealy)

Given all available evidence, historical perspectives and our current treatment choices, which are mainly supportive, PREVENTION is the path of choice. The following are prevention-oriented, holistically sound recommendations for those who are not already carriers:

1–Choose monogamy with a partner who has long been sexually conservative.

2–Avoid all "street" drugs.

3–Avoid anal intercourse, as it weakens the immune system (see paragraph 2 under the section entitled "Transmission of AIDS").

4–Avoid smoking and the use of any tobacco products.

5–Obtain adequate, regular sleep (average 7-8 hours nightly).

6–Eat healthily: avoid fat and sugar. Emphasize whole grains, vegetables and fruits.

7–Exercise regularly. Include exposure to natural sunlight as often as possible. If you ordinarily wear eyeglasses, either take them off when you are outside or use special lenses that allow the full spectrum of light to penetrate the eyes.

8 – Follow a stress-reduction program: 30-40 minutes per day of positive imaging, affirmations and self-regulation, such as biofeedback. You can divide these sessions during the day, such as 15 minutes in the morning and 15 minutes in the evening. Stress-reduction programs are available through most health care centers.

9 – Minimize caffeine and alcoholic beverages.

TREATMENT (Shealy)

Although not fully "proven," the following techniques enhance the immune system and are very safe. Follow the preventive techniques and add the following:

1 – A macrobiotic diet or one very similar

2 – ABSOLUTELY NO SMOKING OR USE OF TOBACCO PRODUCTS

3 – Add slowly to your DAILY nutrition:

Vitamin C (as C-Ascorbates) building over a week or so to 15 grams per day.

Selenium – 100 micrograms

B Complex – 100 milligrams (or take Life Extension Mix R, 9 per day)

Nutri-Logic's Trans-Mins Multimineral complex — 3 per day. (This vitamin is recommended because it is easily absorbed into the body.)

Zinc chelate — 60 milligrams per day

4 — If you can find a physician to administer this, get daily for two weeks the following, administered intravenously:

75 grams Vitamin C

200 milligrams Vitamin B6

1 gram of Magnesium Chloride

1.5 grams Calcium Chloride, all in 500 cc isotonic IV fluid

5 — Use castor oil packs over the entire abdomen all night each night.

The technique for applying castor oil packs is: Soak thoroughly three thicknesses of white wool flannel in castor oil. Cover abdomen from rib cage to pubis, side to side, with the castor-oil soaked flannel. Wrap a large piece of plastic (such as a drycleaning bag) around your entire abdomen and adjacent back. Over that, wrap a large bath towel. Hold the towel in place with a large washable belt (such as from a bathrobe). To hold the pack in place, wear long johns, tights or panty hose and a T-shirt tucked beneath the waistband.

In the morning, remove the pack and wrap in the plastic for reuse. (When reusing, add a small amount of castor oil.) To remove the castor oil, wash yourself with a baking soda solution (2 tbsp. baking soda in one quart of water) or strong soap and water.

6 – Take tincture of Echinacea and tincture of Ligusticum: 5 drops of each four times each day.

7 – Take Colchicine: 0.6 milligrams per day.

8 – If not MUCH better in one month, try Symmetrel-R, 100 milligrams three times per day.

9 – Consider the Seutterman Clinic's homeopathic approach. This clinic is located in Weingarten, West Germany. I have visited there and am very impressed with their approach.

10 – Practice high-quality hatha yoga.

11 – Go to a two- to four-week intensive self-healing training program and learn Biogenics R and past life regression (available through the Shealy Institute, Springfield, MO as well as other holistic health care facilities).

12 – Follow the recommended procedures as described by Caroline Myss for healing one's psychological, emotional and spiritual levels of health. This *attitudinal* healing is more important than *all* other factors combined.

THE JOURNEY OF HEALING (Myss)

Even though I believe that every disease can be healed, I do not believe that the healing of any illness – perhaps especially AIDS – can be accomplished completely through the use of drugs or surgery alone. The traumas of the people who have manifested AIDS indicate that health is generated by a balance of the emotional, psychological and spiritual aspects that form the core of one's being.

The instructions to Peter that I received intuitively in meditation encompassed every area of Peter's life. Peter's healing process was a journey of transformation—of himself, of his way of being, and of his understanding of the power he had to direct the course of his life.

I offer the outline of this journey to those who are undertaking the healing of AIDS so that they also can embark upon such a journey.

In addition to utilizing the nutritional recommendations and the vitamin/mineral supplement program that Norm has described, Peter was directed to heal the negative beliefs that he held of himself—beliefs that resulted from intimidation and pain. Such beliefs render impossible the living of a positively-oriented and productive life.

The process of emotional, psychological and spiritual cleansing that Peter underwent required that he speak openly with his mother and sister, as well as his father, about who he was and about his lifestyle, so that he might release the fear of their rejection of him that had burdened him for so long. Self-acceptance is central to the healing process. Forgiveness of others and of ourselves is also essential to the healing process. No matter how appropriate we consider our anger or resentment, or how unworthy we consider ourselves, these negative feelings do nothing but poison the human body and spirit.

Because Peter was heavily influenced by the morality of a religion that views homosexuality as immoral, Peter was reminded that the morality of humankind does not necessarily reflect the mind of God. The morality of humankind reflects the minds of the people who comprise the society in which one finds oneself. Peter was encouraged to explore his own spirituality.

THE USE OF SEA SALT CRYSTALS

Peter was directed to use sea salt crystals to cleanse the "etheric" (nonphysical) energies in his body which contained the vibration of the AIDS virus. He was told to soak his feet twice a day (preferably morning and evening) in a solution of 3 cups of sea salt crystals in 3 quarts of water, and he was given a visualization to use during the salt soaks. (A recording of this visualization is available through Stillpoint International and it is recommended that the tape be used during the salt soaks.)

The salt water solution can be used for seven days before it needs to be replaced. A pot with a lid, preferably stainless steel or porcelain, can be used as an appropriate container.

RHYTHM OF HEALING AND THE USE OF AFFIRMATIONS

The process of healing has a rhythm that needs reinforcement until the new, positive patterns become natural and automatic. The mind does not easily recognize or respond to new patterns of thinking and feeling that one is in the process of creating, such as a positive self-image. Unless attention is focused continually upon the release of old patterns, and upon the living of new patterns, old patterns resume control of mind and emotions.

For this reason, Peter was instructed to reinforce his positive attitude through the use of 5-minute healing affirmations four times each day: 8 a.m., noon, 4 p.m. and 8 p.m. This cycle strengthens the momentum of the healing process. When you follow this path, let your affirmations reflect the healthy, whole person that you are creating within yourself. Write your affirmations and tape them to walls, a mirror or any place that allows you to see them continually. Let them remind you that you are the generator of your own reality.

COMMITMENT TO THE HEALING PROCESS

Perhaps the most dramatic part of Peter's program was the instruction that *under no circumstance should he allow himself to break the pattern of healing*. No matter how tired, or doubtful, or fearful he became, he was not to relax the recommended procedures for his healing. When he found himself faltering in his commitment, he was directed to employ tools such as meditation or establishing contact with a supportive person, in order to empower himself to continue his efforts.

THE ANCHOR OF MEANING AND
THE SPIRITUAL CONNECTION

At the heart of the journey of healing is the choice to remain within the physical experience of life. The strongest anchor to the physical experience of life is love and a belief that one's life is significant and meaningful. The feeling that one's life is valueless, meaningless and loveless fuels the power of the disease. And yet, value, meaning and love cannot be created upon demand. They emerge from within one's being, when a person is ready to seek them. Prayer, meditation and listening to one's inner guidance are strong medicines. Prayer and introspective thought ignite a level of courage and inner wisdom from which springs forth the natural healing capacity of the human spirit. Ninety percent of human beings say they believe in life after death and in God. Activation of those beliefs and of a sense of purpose is the most important factor anyone can use to create health. In a time of despair, one simple question may serve to initiate hope— "What can I learn from this experience in order to become a more spiritually mature person?"

FINAL THOUGHTS

The AIDS virus will no doubt affect the lives of millions of people throughout this planet. AIDS is not only a challenge to our health care systems, it's a challenge to our humanity. We, as a culture, are already confronting the issue of what to do with children who have AIDS—do we take them out of school? Do we isolate our children or friends and family members who contract the virus? Is isolation the compassionate response, or the fearful one?

If AIDS is, indeed, a virus that thrives on "victim" consciousness, fear responses or support for isolation, legislation cannot produce a positive result. We may not have a vaccine readily available for use in this epidemic, but what we do have is the vaccine which comes from the heart. We have love to give these people along with the other riches of the human experience—we have compassion, hope and understanding.

The crises that are facing us as a planetary family would be met with very different reactions if we could all begin thinking of ourselves as united in our efforts to help heal these problems — it is our environment which is polluted; it is our world that is threatened with nuclear annihilation; it is our family who has AIDS. It is all of us who share these crises — and every one of these crises challenges the way in which we see ourselves in relationship to our world and our participation in this world as members of the same family.

It seems that life has provided us with those situations that will draw from us our highest potential as human beings if we choose from our hearts to respond with love. Love is the only vaccine that can heal these illnesses.

BIOGRAPHICAL MATERIAL

C. Norman Shealy, M.D., Ph.D., is the Director of the Shealy Institute for Comprehensive Pain and Health Care in Springfield, Missouri and President of the Holos Institute of Health. He is Research and Clinical Professor of Psychology, Forest Institute of Psychology. Dr. Shealy has also taught at Harvard, Case Western Reserve, the University of Wisconsin and the University of Minnesota medical schools. He is the author of several books, including the best-selling book *90 DAYS TO SELF-HEALTH* and *THE PAIN GAME*.

Caroline M. Myss, M.A., is Co-Publisher of Stillpoint Publishing, a medical clairvoyant and an international lecturer in the field of human consciousness and health.

PART III:

IN SUMMARY: UNDERSTANDING HOLISTIC TECHNOLOGIES FOR HEALING AND PERSONAL EMPOWERMENT

In Summary

Caroline M. Myss

UNDERSTANDING HOLISTIC TECHNOLOGIES FOR HEALING AND PERSONAL EMPOWERMENT

Most people enter into the holistic world through crisis. For some, it is the crisis of a relationship breakdown. For others, the breakdown of their health is the reason they begin to seek an alternative way of thinking about life. In every case, however, no matter what the particular trauma may be, the person in crisis exists, in that moment, in his or her most vulnerable and weakened condition. Having to seek help, perhaps for the first time, can itself be an overwhelming experience.

The holistic approach to health is only now emerging into our lives. The technologies that reflect a wholistic cosmology are still unfamiliar to many and, therefore, not understood in terms of what makes these technologies effective. The reason for this is that, in general, people do not enter into the healing process already skilled in the practices of visualization, biofeedback, Biogenics, yoga or meditation. In fact, an introduction into these essential skills is often required by people before they can begin to work in an effective way on their own healing.

The following material addresses the most commonly asked questions by people reaching out for an understanding of the holistic journey back to health.

1. WHAT IS MEANT BY THE TERMS WHOLISM AND HOLISM?

Wholism and holism are two terms representing a philosophical view of life which recognizes that all of the systems of life in this universe are interconnected. The terms themselves differ in that the word "holism" is rooted in the word "holy," and therefore absorbs into its definition the spiritual reality of life. It is the *preferred* spelling.

Science has long realized that all the systems of nature are bound intimately to one another and that a major, or even minor, disruption in one system reverberates throughout the other systems of life. For example, consider the systemic effects of pesticides: human life is contaminated, animal life is contaminated and vegetation is contaminated. The contamination absorbed by the vegetation continues its process of poisoning when the food products are later consumed.

2. WHAT DOES HOLISM MEAN AS APPLIED TO HEALTH?

A holistic approach to health or healing begins with the assumption that the "cause" of the illness is directly related to the emotional, psychological and spiritual stress factors present in one's life. The perception of holism recognizes that it is impossible to maintain a strong, healthy physical body if a person lives or works in an environment of continual emotional stress. Prolonged and intense feelings of anger or resentment or fear penetrate the physical body. The process of cause and effect which exists between emotions and physical form is easily recognized when the illness is an ulcer; it is not often as obvious in the instances of cancer or heart disease. Treating the condition of the physical body while disregarding the condition of one's emotions and psychological state cannot effect complete healing. Physical treatment of an illness most often results in a temporary reprieve of an illness. Surgery may be able to remove a tumor, but surgery is incapable of removing the pain of an emotional hurt or trauma. Healing at this level of the illness cannot be done by any health care practitioners. It requires a personal transformation of consciousness to align oneself with one's soul and to work on one's individual purpose in life.

3. WHAT IS NECESSARY TO KNOW ABOUT THE HOLISTIC APPROACH TO HEALING A DISEASE?

In the holistic model of health and healing, it is the *patient* who empowers the healing process, not the physician. Unlike traditional medical treatment—which is "passive" medicine in that drugs or surgery or the physician does the work for you—the holistic approach requires the full participation of the patient in his or her healing process. The holistic approach recognizes that illness is created when emotional, psychological and spiritual stresses become overwhelming, and thus break through into physical manifestation. Complete healing of any physical dysfunction, therefore, must include the healing of one's inner symptoms. Because this level of the healing of the self is crucial, understanding what is meant by "participation" in one's own healing process needs to be addressed.

The most essential shift in awareness a person must ignite on his or her journey of healing is that the technologies of the holistic approach are dependent upon the willingness and capacity of the patient to enter into the discipline of inner work. For so many of us, this process has not been a regular part of our lives. We are not accustomed to giving careful and thoughtful attention to our emotional needs WITH THE INTENTION OF CHANGING WHAT IS NOT HEALTHY, FULFILLING OR SATISFYING TO US. What we are familiar with is REACTING to our emotions. Both a willingness to look deeply into one's inner self and the courage to change that which is not working in our lives are essential to the healing process.

The therapies available to help people in this process are effective ONLY if the person is able first, to recognize the impact of his or her emotional well being on the physical state of the body, and second, to pursue courageously the healing of this level of life. This often requires a complete change of behavior patterns that are familiar and safe, even though they do not create satisfying results. Yet we tend to trust what we know, even if what we know is not working for us. It seems easier at times to believe that we are helpless to change the areas of our lives that are not nurturing to us. The holistic approach to healing does not accommodate the attitude of "helplessness," but, rather, encourages the position that options and choices are always present in one's life, even if these choices hold the possibility of igniting a total transformation of one's life patterns, relationships and occupation.

4. WHAT IS ESSENTIAL TO KNOW ABOUT THE TECHNOLOGIES OF THE HOLISTIC APPROACH TO HEALING?

Very often, a person seeking to create an appropriate healing regimen can become overwhelmed by the abundance of approaches available in the holistic field. Numerous psychotherapy techniques, nutritional programs, homeopathic, naturopathic and acupuncture treatments, as well as biofeedback and visualization techniques, and therapies such as massage and polarity are easily available. And this is only a brief overview. "Is one better than another?" and, "What is right for me?" are questions each person faces as he or she begins to create a healing program.

The most essential question that needs to be asked is, "What do I need to do to heal my whole self?" Before any other choices can be made, every individual must identify the origin of the stress he or she is experiencing in order that the appropriate choices of therapy can be made. It does a person little good, for example, to choose acupuncture treatments when what may be required is a complete evaluation of one's nutritional program. Nor is much assistance found in choosing to alter one's nutritional program if the heart of the problem is a relationship that is not working. And nutrition cannot compensate for the chemical abuse of smoking.

It is also crucial to understand that approaching any of these healing technologies with the attitude that they will, in and of themselves, bring about healing is erroneous. What all of these methods have in common is that the patient empowers the process. No therapist on the planet can help a person who refuses to recognize that certain patterns in his

or her life are not working. A nutritional therapist can provide a person with a health regimen that will produce a balanced physical body, but what good is it if the person chooses
not to stay on the program?

Working with visualization and positive imagery is an
often-recommended technique for helping people to create
a healthy body. Because this technique is so well accepted,
numerous visualizations have been recorded onto cassette
tapes in order that people can work with the process at home.
Yet the tape, in and of itself, has no power. Visualization tapes
are meant to be used as *tools* to assist the activity taking place
within a person's mind. Frequently, people working with this
technique will comment that the tape doesn't work and that
they still have their particular illness. Certainly, several ex-
planations may be forthcoming to explain why a person's
symptoms continue; yet it is worth noting that in many instances, the ineffectual results of someone's visualization practice may rest with the realization that he or she had not been
properly introduced into understanding the basic principles
of this technique. These are worth noting here.

Visualization engages the natural relationship between the
mind and the body to work in harmony. What is transmitted
to the mind as the optimal condition of health through
visualizing an "image" becomes—literally—a working order
to the whole body system. The body responds to the com-
mands of the mind. However, the mind is capable of sending
several "images" simultaneously to the body. A person, may,
for instance, participate in visualization exercises every morning, afternoon and evening with total dedication, focusing
on the mental model of a completely healthy body and yet,
in between those visualization exercises are hours filled with
fear and attention given to the disease. Focusing on the

disease IS ALSO VISUALIZATION. Imaging the disease creates the disease. Imaging health creates health. Therefore, it is crucial to pay attention to the thoughts and fears active in one's mind *at all times,* working to replace them constantly with positive thoughts. It is not enough to engage in a practice of short-term morning and/or evening visualizations and simultaneously live in fear the rest of the day and night. To be effective, positive visualization requires constant focus. It must be applied whenever fears filter into your mind during your healing process.

5. HOW DOES MEDITATION ASSIST THE HEALING PROCESS?

Meditation is the practice of learning to listen to one's inner voice or higher self. Learning to perceive this inner voice requires patience, discipline and a comfortable rapport with silence. Meditation is of great use to the healing process because it assists you in creating a calm emotional state so that you are not continually overwhelmed by every emotion that surfaces during the course of healing. Often, people do not know at first how to enter into a meditation practice. For the beginning student, I recommend finding a reputable teacher, or read literature on the subject which can give you enough confidence to pursue the practice. Meditation tapes are superb tools of assistance for your personal meditation practices.

6. WHAT IS THE BEST ATTITUDE WITH WHICH TO APPROACH MY HEALING PROCESS?

The holistic approach to healing increases in depth and magnitude when it is recognized that *what one is actually choosing is an empowered way of living.* All of the technologies of the alternative treatment field represent the first steps people take toward realizing that each of us can change what is not working for us in our lives, that none of us needs to feel that we are victims of life or of a particular disease, and that we can live life fully and dynamically. No matter what path toward wholeness a person chooses to take, and no matter what specific technologies a person elects to bring into his or her healing regime, they all inevitably lead to the same realization that none of us has to live a life without power and choice. Becoming whole is the final liberation.

APPENDIX:

RECOMMENDED HEALING PRODUCTS FROM STILLPOINT INTERNATIONAL

APPENDIX A
STILLPOINT
INTERNATIONAL, INC.

Books, audio tapes, programs and membership opportunities that give individuals practical ways and techniques to achieve their highest potential in every aspect of their lives.

For a free catalog or ordering information

write:

Stillpoint International, Inc.
Box 640, Walpole, N.H. 03608 USA

or call:

1-800-847-4014 TOLL FREE
(Continental US, except NH)

1-603-756-4225 or 756-3508
(Foreign and NH)

756-9281.

BREAKING THROUGH ILLNESS

IGNITING THE HEALING POWER WITHIN

C. Norman Shealy, M.D., Ph.D.
Caroline M. Myss, M.A.

A complete self-healing program for anyone experiencing illness, stress or a major health or life crisis

Doctors, professional sports trainers, Olympic athletes and, more recently, individuals suffering from debilitating diseases and stress-induced illnesses, have all validated the significance of positive mental images, attitudes and beliefs for achieving superior performance and for creating health. In fact, the alignment of body, mind and spirit, or total self, is the key. BREAKING THROUGH ILLNESS: *Igniting the Healing Power Within,* is a complete self-healing program for anyone experiencing illness, stress or major health or life crisis. It is unique because it guides you into relaxed states of consciousness and into activating your own natural healing powers. Using powerful affirmations, positive mental imagery, and soothing guided meditations, the BREAKING THROUGH ILLNESS program redirects your thoughts in a way that empowers the entire healing process. Each of the six segments of the program (identified below) "ignites the healing power within you" in accordance with universal principles and spirtual laws.

Wise Person Attunement
Power, Responsibility, Wisdom and Love
Transforming Fear
Enhancing Self-Esteem
Every Thought is a Prayer
Healing with Crystalline Energy

This Stillpoint Technologies® tape series for creating health is an effective support system for mastering self-healing techniques. And when you are feeling particularly stressed out, just select the appropriate tape to restore yourself to a state of harmony and balance. In addition to healing, this dynamic program is an excellent "health maintenance system." Used daily, it will help you incorporate life-enhancing thought stimuli into your awareness for creating optimum health.

Cassette album of 3 tapes and instructional guidebook 7 x 10 $29.95

I CHOOSE LIFE

Patricia A. Norris, Ph.D.
and Garrett Porter

I CHOOSE LIFE is an in-depth look at the body's ability to create health through the power of the mind. Dr. Patricia Norris, a gifted psychologist at the Menninger Foundation, explains how visualization, biofeedback and relaxation techniques have been successfully used to promote health and healing. In highlighting her work, Dr. Norris presents 9-year-old Garrett Porter as an example of the extraordinary effectiveness of imagery and biofeedback in the healing process. Garrett was diagnosed with an inoperable brain tumor. In his own words he describes how he worked for a year with biofeedback equipment, special visualizations and relaxation techniques to totally eliminate his tumor. I CHOOSE LIFE is a book for anyone wishing to understand the important role that beliefs, attitudes and expectations play in creating both disease and illness. Dr. Norris clearly explains those methods of visualization which have proven to be highly effective. She discusses:

* **How to take personal responsibility for overcoming one's disease**
* **The relationship between the conscious mind and the unconscious mind in healing**
* **The success of visualization in modern cancer therapy**
* **The importance of a positive attitude with honest and clear intention in creating health**
* **What constitutes the key factors in wellness**
* **How to choose those responses that contribute to sound health**

FOREWORD BY GERALD G. JAMPOLSKY, M.D.

"Garrett Porter is one of a growing number of people who have been able to overcome supposedly fatal diseases. What they all had in common, in addition to their affliction, was a blazing determination."

— *Norman Cousins*
author of ANATOMY OF AN ILLNESS

paper, $10.95   169 pages   ISBN 0-913299-43-X

AGARTHA:
A JOURNEY
TO THE STARS

A STILLPOINT BESTSELLER

"A beautiful illustration of a rapidly growing yet unheralded educational process that may change human consciousness on a global scale."

> Robert A. Monroe
> Author of JOURNEYS OUT OF THE BODY

"I find (AGARTHA) fascinating...it reminds me of the SETH material...and I hope it will reach the many and change their lives enabling them to see life from a different perspective."

> Eileen Caddy
> Author of FOUNDATIONS OF FINDHORN
> and THE DAWN OF CHANGE

AGARTHA: A JOURNEY TO THE STARS is a book of profound wisdom from a perspective beyond the limitations of physical earth and physical reality. It is also a story about intense personal transformation where physical changes, emotional fears and spiritual traumas are explored and shared in a way which sheds light on the awesome experience of meeting one's nonphysical teacher.

Paper, $9.95, 352 pages, 5 1/2 × 8 1/4

AN AGARTHA WORKBOOK

LANGUAGE OF THE SOUL
Applying Universal Principles for Self-Empowerment
Meredith Lady Young

Profound new teachings and practical tools for co-creating with the Universe to maximize your time, talents and spiritual insight

This workbook challenges you to take charge of your life and gives you the practical tools for achieving personal and spiritual growth. It enlightens you to the fact that life at its simplest, truest level is spiritual in nature. By acknowledging this, you learn how to interpret the language of your soul, the pulse of your very being, in order to achieve success in every aspect of your life.

In LANGUAGE OF THE SOUL you will explore major Universal Truths essential to the creation of a meaningful and joyous life. With Mentor, a nonphysical Universal Teacher, instructing you, you will be guided through a process of evaluating your life and choosing that knowledge most relevant to you. Using your natural intuitive skills, you will learn to apply Universal Principles for self-empowerment. As you proceed through the workbook, you will experience the natural process of reaching expanded levels of awareness about who you are and what your relationship to the Universe is. Through your intuitive perceptions, you will discover your own greatest source of knowledge and creativity. In so doing, you will learn to co-create with the Universe to become all that you can be.
Paper, $12.50, 156 pages, 8 1/2 × 11 oversize format.

LANGUAGE OF THE SOUL speaks directly to the unmet needs within us today. This workbook challenges us to find our higher purpose in our journey to understanding ourselves. Its magic is that it puts theory into practical application in our daily lives. Its gift is that by using this workbook we are empowered to heal ourselves. It is the medicine of the future here right now.

Bruce F. Middendorf, M.D.
Director of Outpatient Department
Millard-Fillmore Hospital
Buffalo, New York

LANGUAGE OF THE SOUL represents a practical and useful tool for us to bring the theory of Universal Truths into our daily lives. It provides us with a way of seeing our lives more clearly, empowering us to truly live as we speak.

Donna Sommers, R.N.
Editor, Balance Magazine
Branford, Connecticut

In LANGUAGE OF THE SOUL, Meredith Young has a remarkable way of letting people know there is something powerful within each of them. More than helping others see this inner strength, she shows how to personally experience and draw on it in everyday life.

Jim Rousmaniere
Editor and President
The Keene Sentinel
Keene, New Hampshire

In LANGUAGE OF THE SOUL, you will explore major Universal Truths essential to the creation of a meaningful and joyous life.

Commit To A Vision Through Personal Action

JOIN

THE CO-CREATORS

THE CO-CREATORS are individuals who want to see their lives from a much broader perspective, and who truly desire to make wise choices based on a new way of being. They are men and women who acknowledge that to change society we must first change ourselves.

MEMBERSHIP OPPORTUNITY

ACTIVE MEMBER

A 1-year Membership entitles you to:

• The CO-CREATORS Membership Card
Identifies you as an individual committed to personal growth and self empowerment in order to create a better world.

• A Magnificent Channeled Tape from the Universal Teachers, Mentor and Genesis
They will share their thoughts from their expanded perspective on the role and responsibility of human beings to evolve to the next level of consciousness in order to build an empowered world of peace and unity.

• Your Personal Copy of EITHER the New AGARTHA Workbook, LANGUAGE OF THE SOUL, by Meredith Lady Young, OR

The bestselling Book AGARTHA: A Journey to the Stars by Meredith Lady Young

• A 15% Discount on All Stillpoint Products
(Except those already at special prices)

• The Complete CO-CREATION COURSE I, Applying Universal Principles for Self-Empowerment, (see following pages for description of Program), OR

The Complete CO-CREATION COURSE II, Applying Universal Principles for Spiritual Fitness (see following pages for description of Program).

Select one of the above Stillpoint Technologies Programs.

• Selected Channeled Information from Mentor and Genesis on Topical Subjects that can Dramatically Affect Your Life (Released as appropriate.)

Call or write STILLPOINT for membership application.

VISION SUPPORTER
A 1-year membership entitles you to:

• The CO-CREATORS Membership Card
• A Magnificent Channeled Tape from the Universal Teachers, Mentor and Genesis
• Your Personal Copy of EITHER the New AGARTHA Workbook, LANGUAGE OF THE SOUL, by Meredith Lady Young
OR
The bestselling Book AGARTHA: A Journey to the Stars, by Meredith Lady Young

• Selected Channeled Information from Mentor and Genesis on Topical Subjects that can Dramatically Affect Your Life (Released as appropriate.)

• A 15% Discount on all Stillpoint Products
(Except those already at special prices.)

Call or write STILLPOINT for membership application.

CO-CREATION COURSE I APPLYING UNIVERSAL PRINCIPLES FOR SELF-EMPOWERMENT

This interactive audio tape series and personal journal has been a remarkably successful self-study program in the series of STILLPOINT Technologies© courses produced to empower the individual.

APPLYING UNIVERSAL PRINCIPLES FOR SELF-EMPOWERMENT is a unique course which includes six instructional audio tapes, journal pages with experiential exercises and a course Guide Book. It was created by Meredith Lady Young, author of the bestselling book, *Agartha: A Journey to the Stars* and Mentor, a Universal Teacher.

This program takes you through a process of personal experiential understanding that many course participants have described as, "truly enlightening and capable of producing new skills in perception, intuition and channeling.

Young and Mentor skillfully teach you major Universal Truths and Spiritual Laws that are personally relevant and meaningful. You will explore your inner and outer worlds and gain a vast new perspective of your unlimited potential.

You will be shown how to evaluate your life and choose that knowledge which will enhance every aspect of your life. You will be guided in the ways to use your natural skills (intuition, higher-self guidance and channeling) to reach beyond your current level of creative ability in order to draw to yourself the immense cooperative energy of the Universe.

You will learn, in practical terms, how to apply Universal Principles to produce the greatest harmony in your life. You will learn how to Listen and Respond and Act in the ways most appropriate to your life.

MONTH	COURSE/SUBJECT AREA
1	Intuitive Searching (channeling) – Experiencing a Vast Universe
2	Expectations of Living: Seasons of the Body, Mind and Spirit
3	Understanding your Relationship to Physical Reality
4	The Influence of Love
5	Spirituality and the Language of the Universe
6	Nothing but Oneness

A STILLPOINT Technologies© self-study educational course. Course album with 6 instructional cassettes, journal pages with experiential exercises and course guide book. $89.95*

Note*: Price is subject to change at any time.

CO-CREATION COURSE II APPLYING UNIVERSAL PRINCIPLES FOR SPIRITUAL FITNESS

This second self-study program in the series of STILLPOINT Technologies© courses parallels the highly successful teaching structure of Co-Creation Course I.

APPLYING UNIVERSAL PRINCIPLES FOR SPIRITUAL FITNESS combines interactive audio tapes with a personal journal to take you through a highly effective process of experiential learning and self-assessment. This powerful course includes six instructional audio tapes, journal pages with experiential exercises and a Course Guide Book. Caroline Myss, who has worked extensively with Dr. Norman Shealy (well-known neurosurgeon and founder of The American Holistic Medical Association), and Genesis, a Universal Teacher, are the principle authors of this program.

By understanding the Universal Principles of how you create health (or disease), you will learn to skillfully apply these laws and your natural abilities in the optimum way. Through the guidance of Myss and Genesis you will challenge existing belief patterns and attitudes in order to move past limitations and into wholeness. You will learn to quickly identify how stress is triggered in your body by emotional, psychological or spiritual imbalance and then how to consciously reverse it.

APPLYING UNIVERSAL PRINCIPLES FOR SPIRITUAL FITNESS offers you practical guidance and instruction for achieving total fitness of body, mind and spirit.

MONTH	COURSE/SUBJECT AREAS
1	Shifting to Holistic Consciousness: Creating the Foundation for Health
2	Power/Responsibility/Wisdom/Love: The Learning Lessons of Life
3	Understanding and Applying the Co-Creative Dynamics which Create Health
4	Challenging Your Personal Belief Systems
5	Creating a Spiritual Partnership with the Universe
6	Igniting Your Spirit: Tipping the Balance for Global Transformation

A STILLPOINT Technologies© self-study educational course. Course album with 6 instructional cassettes, journal pages with experiential exercises and course guide book. $89.95*

Note*: Price is subject to change at any time.

Aids - Biologically Speaking
P. 75 ⇒.